U.S. HISTORY

HISTORIC EVENTS, KEY PEOPLE, IMPORTANT LOCATIONS, AND MORE!

101

KATHLEEN SEARS

Adams Media

New York   London   Toronto   Sydney   New Delhi

Adams Media
An Imprint of Simon & Schuster, Inc.
100 Technology Center Drive
Stoughton, MA 02072

For information about special discounts for bulk purchases, please contact Simon & Schuster Special Sales at 1-866-506-1949 or business@simonandschuster.com.

The Simon & Schuster Speakers Bureau can bring authors to your live event. For more information or to book an event contact the Simon & Schuster Speakers Bureau at 1-866-248-3049 or visit our website at www.simonspeakers.com.

Manufactured in the United States of America

6 2023

Library of Congress Cataloging-in-Publication Data has been applied for.

ISBN 978-1-4405-8648-4
ISBN 978-1-4405-8649-1 (ebook)

Contains material adapted and abridged from *The Everything® American History Book, 2nd Edition* by John R. McGeehan, copyright © 2007 by Simon & Schuster, Inc., ISBN 978-1-59869-261-7, and *The Everything® American Revolution Book* by Daniel P. Murphy, copyright © 2008 by Simon & Schuster, Inc., ISBN 978-1-59869-538-0.

CONTENTS

INTRODUCTION

The United States is a great experiment.

When the Founding Fathers gathered in Philadelphia first in 1776 to hammer out the reasons for the colonies' separation from England and then in 1789 to agree on a form of government for the new nation they'd brought into being, they were fully aware of the unusual nature of what they were doing. True, there had been revolutions in history before. But no one before this had undertaken to so radically reform the nature of society, to create from scratch a country governed by its people, one in which "all men are created equal."

That vision has taken a long time to realize, and it's not yet complete. Perhaps it never will be. America's history has been punctuated by a long, bloody civil war, unrest and rebellion, physical expansion and political turmoil, and by economic growth and contraction. Today, as the most powerful nation on Earth, the United States continues its experiment in freedom.

This book was written to help you understand and appreciate that experiment. In its sixty-three entries, you'll find information about events ranging from the landing of Columbus to the Great Recession; from the Boston Massacre to the Boston Marathon bombing.

Sometimes, because we often take history for granted, it's possible to lose track of the power and meaning of the story of the United States. For all its flaws—and many of them will be pointed out in the pages that follow—America is a remarkable country. This rapid journey through its history will let you glance at both the high and low points and see how they contribute to the totality.

U.S. History 101 doesn't dwell in detail on any single topic; rather, it lets you skim through American history and see where the country's been—and possibly get an indication of where it might be going.

Take a moment to look at a dollar bill. On the back of the bill, on the left side, you'll see the Great Seal of the United States, adopted toward the end of the revolution. At the bottom of the seal appears a quote adapted from the poet Virgil: "*Novus Ordo Seclorum*." The phrase means, "a new order of the ages." That's how the founders of the United States saw their revolution—as a decisive break from the past. As the heirs of and participants in that new age, we need to understand and value its history.

CROSSING THE LAND BRIDGE

The First People

Long before the arrival of Christopher Columbus, the American continents had been home to a thriving indigenous population of perhaps 70 to 90 million people for more than 20,000 years. The first humans to inhabit North America probably arrived from Asia by land bridge or sea, long before European contact.

BERINGIA

Some 35,000 years ago, when much of the northern oceans were massive glaciers and ocean levels were much lower, the Bering Strait land bridge connected northern Asia and what is now Alaska. Although we refer to it as a bridge, it was in reality a large body of land, called Beringia, that connected the two continents and was home for around 5,000 years to a number of human beings. At some point (evidence is sharply divided on when this occurred) these humans began moving east and south, gradually spreading across the North American continent.

Archaeologists and anthropologists generally agree that most of the people native to North America migrated from Siberia, likely pursuing animals such as the woolly mammoth. These people gradually spread to Central and South America. Ilya Zakharov, deputy director of Moscow's Vavilov Institute of General Genetics, has conducted DNA testing to determine the exact origin of North American Native Americans. In an expedition he led in 1997, Zakharov went to the Ak-Dovurak region, 2,000 miles southeast of Moscow, and took hair samples from about 430 Tuvan people. An analysis of the DNA contained in the hair root was compared with Inuit and Amerindian, including Navajo and Apache, samples. High percentages of exact matches of the DNA between the Tuvan samples and those of Native Americans support the link between Siberia and North American peoples.

Multiple Origins?

Even though anthropologists generally agree that the land bridge was a major source of the first inhabitants of North America, some evidence suggests that parts of the population may have come from elsewhere. For instance, the fossilized skulls of the Beringians look quite different from those of Mesoamericans from the south. It's possible that these people arrived by boat from some unknown location.

LEIF ERICSON AND VINLAND

The Vikings Make Landfall

Although there are a number of theories—some supported by archae-ological evidence—concerning early voyages to the Americas, the most accepted one concerns the people known as the Vikings.

Evidence suggests that around the year 1000, the Norse explorer Leif Ericson, the second son of Eric the Red, who had landed in Greenland in 982, set foot on the North American shore, which he called Vinland (later called Newfoundland) for its profusion of what he referred to as wild grapes. Legend tells that he fitted out an expe-dition and sailed west, in an attempt to gather proof of the claims made by the Icelandic trader Bjarni Herjulfsson. In 986 Herjulfsson, driven far off course by a fierce storm between Iceland and Green-land, had reported sighting hilly, heavily forested land far to the west. Herjulfsson, though likely the first European to see the continent of North America, never set foot on its shores.

In 1960, archaeologists discovered the remains of an ancient settlement at L'Anse aux Meadows on the very northern tip of Newfoundland in Canada. Investigation established that this was a Norse settlement, which many have identified with Leif Ericson and Vinland (though Vinland seems to have referred to the whole land and not just the area in which the Norse settled).

The outpost at L'Anse aux Meadows lasted only a few years; although the Norse found plenty of fish and birds to sustain them, the absence of large game forced them to turn their interest elsewhere, and they abandoned the settlement.

Adam of Bremen and Vinland

The German medieval historian Adam of Bremen (second half of the eleventh century) reported that he had been informed of the Norse discovery of North America. In his chronicle, he writes: "[Svend Estridsen, the Danish ruler] also told me of another island discovered by many in that ocean. It is called Vinland because vines grow there on their own accord, producing the most excellent wine. Moreover, that unsown crops abound there, we have ascertained not from fabulous conjecture but from the reliable reports of the Danes."

COLUMBUS'S VOYAGES

Europeans Discover America by Accident

In fourteen hundred and ninety-two, as every schoolchild knows, Columbus sailed the ocean blue. There have been a lot of myths about Columbus's voyage.

Myth: Columbus proved the world was round, not flat.
Fact: He did no such thing, since he didn't circumnavigate the globe. Nor did he need to; by the fifteenth century, pretty much all educated people knew the world was round.

Myth: Columbus discovered the New World.
Fact: As we've seen, the Vikings had already landed there—not to mention that there had been people living in the Americas for at least 20,000 years before Columbus arrived.

Christopher Columbus was born near Genoa, in Northern Italy, in 1451. Young Columbus began his seafaring career shortly after Portuguese navigators reached the Cape Verde Islands off the coast of West Africa in 1460.

COLUMBUS HAD A HUNCH

Around 1483, Columbus went to King John II of Portugal for endorsement of his plan to discover a new route to Asia by sailing west. Asia was the place to get what everyone wanted back then—spices, essential for preserving food. But King John II rejected Columbus's petition. By 1485 and now a widower, Columbus moved with his son to Spain. Persistent as ever, he presented a plan the following year to Isabella and Ferdinand, the queen and king of Spain. Again, Columbus was refused. However, in 1489 Queen Isabella listened to Columbus again. He left their meeting with hopes of organizing a future expedition, once Spain's war with the Moors was over.

READY, SET, SAIL

In 1492 the Spanish sovereigns approved Columbus's expedition to find a western route to Asia on behalf of Spain. Preparations in the Spanish port of Palos began in May with the requisitioning of three ships, and by August the *Niña*, *Pinta*, and *Santa María* set sail. Columbus was commissioned with the promise that he would receive one-tenth of the profits from the expeditions, and he was granted several titles, including "Admiral of the Ocean Sea," viceroy, and governor of whatever lands he discovered.

First to Get the Reward

Ferdinand and Isabella had promised that the first man to sight land would get a yearly pension of 10,000 *maravedis* (Spanish gold coin). A few hours after midnight on October 12, 1492, Juan Rodriguez Bermeo, a lookout on the *Pinta*, spotted what was most likely an island of the Bahamas, but Columbus claimed to have spied land first and collected the reward himself.

After taking on supplies in the Canary Islands and sailing over the vast sea, on October 12, 1492, crewmembers sighted land. The natives they encountered called the land Guanahani, which Columbus later dubbed San Salvador. Historians still argue about the precise landing spot, but it was somewhere in the Bahamas.

COLUMBUS MISCALCULATED

Columbus believed he had found Asia, but actually he'd miscalculated the distance, and a few other minor details. In fact, to say he misjudged would be an understatement. Some believe he underestimated Earth's size by 25 percent. Many people, including Columbus, thought the oceans were far smaller than they really are and that the land masses were much larger. His crew wasn't pleased that their journey took as long as it did, and there were rumblings of mutiny.

Believing he'd landed in Asia, or the Indies, Columbus called the natives he encountered "Indians." Since he hadn't found the spices he was looking for, he kept sailing, encountering Cuba and Hispaniola (modern-day Haiti and the Dominican Republic). In a Christmas Day storm, the *Santa María* struck a coral reef, split open, and sank in the vicinity of today's Cap-Haïtien in Haiti.

THE FIRST COLONY

Columbus didn't know what to do with the survivors of the *Santa María*. The *Pinta* wasn't nearby, and the *Nina*, the smallest of the fleet, could not make room for the *Santa María*'s crew. In the end, Columbus decided to leave behind thirty-nine of his men to establish a colony he named La Navidad (Christmas), the first attempt at European settlement since the Vikings.

These European settlers discovered not only a new land, but new ways of living and eating as well. For instance, the Arawak (Bahamas) and Taíno (Caribbean) slept in hand-woven *hamacas*, or hammocks. Columbus's men discovered a new diet of corn (maize), sweet potatoes, and red chili pepper, and they learned to grow squash, pumpkins, and beans. Then there was the botanical novelty the inhabitants smoked—tobacco. In turn, the Arawak learned how to farm with cattle, pigs, and horses, which the Europeans later brought with them. However, the Native Americans had no resistance to European diseases, and many succumbed to smallpox, whooping cough, and measles. Diseases brought to the Caribbean by the Europeans contributed to the deaths of more than 3 million Native Americans between 1494 and 1508.

Return with Natives

Columbus sailed home triumphantly, bringing several Native Americans as proof of his successful expedition. While in Lisbon, he wrote a soon-to-be-famous letter describing his Caribbean discoveries, and shortly thereafter appeared in Spain before Queen Isabella and King Ferdinand.

COLUMBUS RETURNS

After an absence of six and a half years, the *Pinta* reappeared in Hispaniola. When Columbus had departed years before, he'd left La Navidad unfortified, for he assumed the relations between his settlers and the Native Americans were amicable. Little did he suspect that the Spaniards would take to pillaging and plundering, and that the once-friendly Native Americans would retaliate. No doubt some colonists also succumbed to illness and perhaps were unaccustomed to the tropical climate. On his return voyage in 1493, Columbus found no survivors at the settlement.

Seventeen caravels (fast sailing ships) with nearly 1,200 men sailed as part of Columbus's second expedition. He set a more southerly course this time, aiming for unexplored islands he'd learned about, including Dominica, Guadeloupe, Puerto Rico, and Jamaica.

Unhappy that his first settlement site had been dictated by the shipwreck, Columbus chose to sail east to establish another new colony. But this time weather was a deterring factor. With trade winds so strong he could not safely continue sailing, he chose another site for his new settlement (still on Hispaniola), which he named La Isabela.

The *Ecomienda* System

In the *ecomienda* system, the Spanish conquistadors were given trusteeship over the native people they conquered. The conquistador could tax his trustees and summon them for labor on the land and in return he was to provide law and order and teachings in Catholicism. The system however was quickly corrupted and became a tool for oppression, ultimately forcing the natives into slavery.

Even after all this time, Columbus still believed that Cuba was a part of the Asian mainland and that he wasn't far off his original course. However, he was discouraged to find none of the golden treasures that Marco Polo had described from his journeys in Asia.

POOR MANAGEMENT

Rather than sending gold back to the Spanish court, Columbus captured natives, sending them home to be sold as slaves. The Crown also authorized the *encomienda* system, which, instead of being a grant of land, was a grant of a type of slave labor. The natives revolted, skirmishes ensued at the colony, and Queen Isabella objected to the slaves, sending a royal commission to investigate the situation. Because of the criticism he received, Columbus established a new capital, calling it Santo Domingo. He then retreated to Spain to plan yet a third voyage.

THE FINAL VOYAGES

Competition among the explorers was intense. Portugal had sent Vasco da Gama on an expedition in 1497. Unlike Columbus, da Gama really did reach India in 1498. It's thought that this provided the impetus for the sovereigns to approve a third journey for the admiral.

A Speed Record

For his third trip, Columbus organized the entire fleet in roughly four weeks, with the goal of circumnavigating the world. He left on May 9, 1502, only three months after the new "Governor of the Indies" had been sent off, but he was forbidden to return to Hispaniola.

On Columbus's third journey, he uncovered Venezuela and the islands of Trinidad and Margarita, and again visited Hispaniola, only to find revolts against his brother's rule. In 1500, in an effort to restore order and peace, Queen Isabella and King Ferdinand sent another governor to Hispaniola. Columbus was arrested and sent back to Spain. Somehow he managed to finagle authorization to undertake a fourth voyage.

Columbus explored the Central American coast for nearly six months in search of the westward passage that remained elusive. He attempted to establish a gold-mining camp in Panama. The natives thwarted these plans, however. He and his men explored Martinique briefly and were shipwrecked off Jamaica, where they remained for a year awaiting rescue.

Finally a ship sent from Hispaniola rescued them. Columbus then set sail for Spain, where he arrived in poor health. During his audience with King Ferdinand (the queen had died), he was rebuffed; the king revoked the admiral's rights and titles. On May 20, 1506, Christopher Columbus died, still hanging on to the notion that he'd reached Asia.

NATIVE AMERICANS

The Original Inhabitants

It's impossible to know exactly how many people were living in North America at the time of Columbus's arrival in 1492, but it was probably in the region of 25 million. They had, by this time, developed a wide variety of cultures and languages—possibly up to 2,000 tongues were spoken by Native Americans—and had spread across the continent.

Some tribes wandered and survived by hunting and gathering, as had Columbus's distant ancestors in Europe, Asia, and the Middle East. Others settled in one place. They grew corn and hunted native animals, particularly the buffalo, which roamed the Western plains in enormous numbers. They built houses in some places; for example, the Zuni and Hopi tribes in the Southwest constructed cliff dwellings clinging to the sides of mountains for protection and shelter. They developed styles of art that were reflected in their sculptures and textiles.

The Moundbuilders

From about 3600 B.C. to the time of Columbus, Native American tribes in the Ohio Valley created a series of enormous earthen mounds. These were generally religious in their purpose, but they also expressed the tribes' artistic visions. Some were shaped like animals. In these mounds, the people left artifacts, including jewelry, clothing, pottery, and other objects.

The tribes had complex social structures. The Iroquois of what is now upstate New York bound themselves into a powerful confederacy that made them the most important tribe on the East Coast. It has been widely speculated that the Iroquois tribal structure was one of the examples the framers of the Constitution had in mind when they drew up their historic document.

Among the Iroquois, much property was held in common, and there was little division between the sexes.

This isn't to say that Native American society was a utopia. Tribes could and did go to war with one another; power struggles between them were frequent. But in general they preserved a peace among themselves and found a niche in the nature that surrounded them.

In one important respect, they were very different from the Europeans: they had no written language. Stories and legends of the tribe were passed down orally from generation to generation. Songs, poetry, all were transmitted by word of mouth. It's for this reason that in many cases we know so little about them. Sadly, they were about to meet a force that within a century would begin to push them back farther and farther until at last there was nowhere else to go.

MAJOR NATIVE AMERICAN TRIBES

Among the most significant Native American tribes are:

- Algonquin
- Apache
- Blackfoot
- Cherokee
- Cheyenne
- Chippewa
- Choctaw
- Comanche
- Creek
- Hopi
- Iroquois
- Miami
- Navajo
- Nez Perce
- Ottawa
- Pawnee
- Sioux
- Ute
- Wampanoag
- Yaqui

JAMESTOWN

A Permanent North American Settlement

In 1605, two groups of London merchants who had combined the investments of many smaller investors petitioned King James I for a charter to establish another colony in Virginia. These two groups—prototypes of modern-day corporations—became the Virginia Company of London and the Plymouth Company.

After receiving its charter, the Virginia Company organized its expedition, providing free passage to America in exchange for a contract under which the settlers agreed to seven years of indentured servitude. This became a popular arrangement. In December 1606, those who signed on (numbering about 100) boarded three vessels—the *Susan Constant*, the *Discovery*, and the *Godspeed*.

UNDER WAY

By May 1607, the 104 remaining settlers commanded by Captain Christopher Newport sailed their three frail vessels through the Chesapeake Bay and thirty miles up the James River to reach a parcel of densely wooded, swampy land. There, the settlers built Jamestown, England's first permanent North American colony.

They arrived too late in the season to plant crops, and the swamps didn't help their chances of survival. Many of these genteel souls were not accustomed to manual labor. Everyone had to carve out homes in the wilderness, where there was no choice but to adapt. Many did not. Within a few months, some settlers died of famine and disease, while others went to live with Native American tribes. Only thirty-eight made it through their first year in the New World.

That these settlers survived at all is due in large measure to Captain John Smith, a former crusader and pirate turned gentleman. Smith turned the settlers into foragers and successful traders with the Native Americans, who taught the English how to plant corn and other crops.

JOHN SMITH AND POCAHONTAS

During an expedition to explore the regions surrounding Jamestown, the chief of the Powhatan Native Americans captured Smith. According to an account Smith published in 1624, he was going to be put to death until the chief's daughter, Pocahontas, saved him. (Pocahontas's real name was Matoaka. The Native American name "Pocahontas" means "playful one.") From this the legend of Pocahontas sprang forth, becoming part of American folklore, children's books, and videos. But did it really happen?

Interracial Marriage in Early Virginia

In their very first years in Virginia, the British encouraged interracial marriage with the Native Americans in order to promote better relations. In Virginia, money was offered to white Virginians who would marry Native Americans. Few took advantage of the offer and later the English would forbid interracial marriage. Pocahontas would be one of the last Native Americans to be accepted into British-American society through marriage.

Some historians say Smith did not mention this Native American woman or his release in any of the documents he wrote about the colony's first year. Smith's account of the capture was published long after the supposed event took place, which leads some historians to believe Smith was just trying to create a good story. In 1614, Smith returned to America, exploring and mapping the New England coast. He later sailed back to England with valuable furs and fish and became a prolific writer and supporter of American colonization.

Evidence is scarce that Pocahontas actually helped John Smith, risking her life to save him. The Jamestown settlers did capture a young Pocahontas around 1612, returning her to their colony. In captivity, she caught the eye of John Rolfe, an Englishman, who later married her with the blessing of her father and the English governor. This established a peace with the Powhatan that lasted eight years. Pocahontas converted to Christianity and took the name Rebecca. In 1615, she gave birth to her first child, Thomas.

With his bride and new son, Rolfe returned to England. Just as she was preparing to return to Virginia in 1617, Pocahontas died of smallpox and was buried in the chapel of the parish church in Gravesend, England.

THE TOP CROP

Although Pocahontas won the hearts of the English, tobacco also captured their attention. It was a primary reason behind the Jamestown settlement's success. In fact, Jamestown became the capital of Virginia.

Moreover, the tobacco crop attracted more settlers to the colonies, where they planted it in every available inch of fertile soil. But once indentured servitude ended, settlers were hard-pressed to maintain their tobacco and other crops. So, they began purchasing laborers from Dutch traders who kidnapped black Africans in their homelands, transported them against their will across the ocean, and sold them to plantation owners—the start of slavery in America.

Relations with the Native Americans began to sour, for the natives frequently attacked Jamestown. In 1622, 350 colonists were killed. By 1644, a total of 500 had perished. A rebellion against the governor resulted in the burning of the settlement. Middle Plantation, in what is now Williamsburg, became the seat of colonial government in 1699, and Jamestown was deserted.

THE DUTCH, FRENCH, AND SPANISH ARRIVE

Among other early European influences on the Americas were the Dutch, the French, and the Spanish.

In 1609 the Dutch East India Company commissioned English explorer Henry Hudson to find a northwest passage across the Atlantic Ocean to India. Hudson entered New York Bay and sailed partway up what is now known as the Hudson River. In 1614 Adriaen Block, another Dutch explorer, navigated the East River. The Dutch monarchy claimed the island of Manhattan and its environs, naming them New Amsterdam.

The French, starting in the sixteenth century, began with the same viewpoint as Columbus and the Dutch: North America was really just an obstacle to finding a sea path to the Indies. The French sent several expeditions to explore the land between Newfoundland

and Florida and wound up establishing a permanent settlement in what is now Quebec City. The French also established a major settlement on the Caribbean island of Hispaniola.

Spain's early conquests were in Mexico, where Hernán Cortéz destroyed the civilization of the Aztecs in central Mexico. After that, Spanish influence and control spread across South America and into the southwest sections of North America. In 1513, Vasco Núñez de Balboa crossed the Isthmus of Panama and finally found the Pacific Ocean, for which explorers since Columbus had been searching.

THE MAYFLOWER COMPACT

The Puritans at Plymouth

In the mid-sixteenth century, during the reign of Elizabeth I, reformers complained that the Protestant Church of England resembled the Catholic Church too closely for comfort. Because this group wanted to purify the church, they became known as the Puritans.

Hard times had fallen on England, and these reformers suffered greatly from the ills of a bad economy with high unemployment and low wages. The Puritans blamed their lot on the Church of England. King James I, who succeeded Elizabeth I, did not take well to their outspokenness.

Although most Puritans believed they could change the church and still belong to it, others chose to create a separate congregation outside of the established church. They became known as the Separatists and suffered harsh treatment—which included not being able to attend universities or worship openly. Separatists were imprisoned and sometimes put to death.

A good many of these Separatists escaped to the Netherlands, where some became sailors aboard Dutch merchant ships. Others returned to England in 1620, but were still unhappy. The New World in America that people spoke of was simply too enticing to pass up. In a new land, the Separatists could worship as they pleased, create a truly religious society, and yet retain their English identity. It was this group that made up the core of the Pilgrims.

STRANGERS AMONG THEM

Planning their voyage, the Pilgrims recruited a number of others to join them. Approximately eighty "strangers," who weren't Separatists or Puritans, decided to sail as well, seeking better lives, adventure, shipboard jobs, and, of course, great wealth. Among these men were Captain Miles Standish and John Alden.

The group, intending to sail on two ships, had obtained a charter to settle in the Virginia Colony. Their ships, the *Speedwell* and the *Mayflower*, were outfitted for their Atlantic crossings. Twice during the summer months they set sail, and twice they returned to England because the *Speedwell* wasn't seaworthy. So the *Mayflower* headed out alone, sailing from Plymouth, England, in September 1620.

The *Mayflower* spent two months crossing an angry Atlantic Ocean. To make matters worse, inaccurate maps and strong winds took the sailors well north of the Virginia Colony. On November 21, 1620, the Pilgrims reached Provincetown Harbor at the tip of Cape Cod, Massachusetts.

SIGNING THE COMPACT

Although the *Mayflower*'s passengers were happy to reach dry land, they were also concerned because their charter from the London merchants had sent them to Virginia. Some of the strangers aboard talked of breaking away from the group. Noting the dissension among them, the passengers drew up an agreement while anchored in the harbor. The Mayflower Compact was the first colonial agreement that formed a government by the consent of those governed. The signers agreed to follow all "just and equal" laws that the settlers enacted. Furthermore, the majority would rule in matters where there was disagreement. The Mayflower Compact guided the colonists until they joined with the Massachusetts Bay Colony in 1691.

NATIVE AMERICAN AID AT PLYMOUTH COLONY

When the Pilgrims established Plymouth Colony, they chose this site for its farm fields, its supply of fresh drinking water, and the hill that enabled them to build a fort. But by early 1621, the Pilgrims were cold, hungry, and sick. They had arrived too late to plant crops, and with the snow, cold, and dwindling food supply, as many as half the colonists died.

The hope of spring kept them going. So did a surprise in the form of a Native American named Samoset, who entered their settlement, speaking English. Soon he brought Squanto, another Native American friend and part of the tribe that had lived at Plymouth before the colonists' arrival, to serve as their guide, teaching them how to survive with new methods of farming and fishing. The Pilgrims learned to plant corn, fertilize their fields, and prosper in other ways as well.

Thanksgiving

Native Americans had celebrated autumn harvests for centuries. Early New Englanders celebrated Thanksgiving only when there was a plentiful harvest, but it gradually became an annual custom. During the American Revolution, the Continental Congress proposed a national day of thanksgiving, and in 1863, Abraham Lincoln issued the proclamation designating the fourth Thursday in November as Thanksgiving Day.

Squanto acted as the interpreter between the Pilgrims and the great Chief Massasoit of the Wampanoag in southeastern Massachusetts. The two sides pledged not to harm one another, and by the following autumn in 1621, the Pilgrims celebrated their first harvest with their Native American neighbors. Both brought provisions for that first Thanksgiving feast, which lasted three days.

The feast probably included:

- Venison
- Wild turkeys
- Cornmeal
- Lobster
- Mussels

THE SALEM WITCH TRIALS

A Town Gone Mad

Because their beliefs were based on independent congregations, free of the church hierarchy that existed back in England, the settlers became known as Congregationalists. Attendance at Sunday services was mandatory, and with the work required to thrive in the colonies, that left little leisure time. There was no dancing, no real recreation. Ironically, life was reminiscent of the past oppression of the Puritans. The punishment for any crime committed was harsh, and those who spoke out against the puritanical dictates were persecuted. Indeed, the Puritans proved to be as intolerant as the king they had fled.

In 1684, England revoked the Massachusetts Bay Colony's charter, and in 1691, the colony was granted a new royal charter that essentially ended the form of government the Puritans had created. The right to elect representatives was now based on property qualifications rather than church membership. The hysteria and wild accusations in Salem in 1692 further eroded the Puritanical influence.

WITCHCRAFT!

In 1692 in Salem Village (modern-day Danvers) two girls—nine-year-old Betty Parris and her eleven-year-old cousin Abigail Williams—caused a stir, not only in the home of the Reverend Samuel Parris, but in the town of Salem itself.

Betty and Abigail began acting strangely, running around the house, flapping their arms, screaming, and throwing themselves around the room. Local doctors were at a loss to explain their antics and fell back on a diagnosis of witchcraft.

Betty and Abigail identified the Parris family's West Indian slave, Tituba, as their tormentor, before adding other names such as Sarah Good and Sarah Osborne. As a black slave, Tituba was already at a disadvantage, while Sarah Good was vulnerable to such accusations because she was homeless, and Sarah Osborne's morals were already in question because she did not attend church.

Executions and Aftermath

Nineteen people were executed in the wake of the Salem Witch Trials, until public opinion turned against the accusers and local judges. In 1696, the General Court adopted a resolution of repentance. Although the Puritan influence declined, the Congregational churches remained dominant in Massachusetts into the nineteenth century.

Many more of Salem's teenage girls began having fits, and the finger pointing continued. Thus it was a true "witch hunt" and persecution of the worst kind.

CAUSES OF THE HYSTERIA

There have been many debates about the causes of the witch hysteria in Salem in the seventeenth century. Some historians suggest that the events were about land and that certain families in the village were attempting to seize property by accusing the owners of witchcraft. Others maintain that the conflict reflected longstanding feuds and conflicts, typical of village life in America and elsewhere.

Accusations of witchcraft were widespread in Europe and America during the seventeenth century. Between 1645–1663, eighty people in the Massachusetts Bay Colony were accused of witchcraft, so from one standpoint the wave of accusations in Salem wasn't that unusual.

Other historians have cited the Salem events as an example of the tensions that underlay colonial and post-colonial America. Slavery, of course, was a festering sore on the American body politic from early on, but there were many indentured servants and other people who were excluded from political and social life who expressed their rebellion in various ways. The events of Salem and elsewhere may have been a reflection of those social conflicts.

Bacon's Rebellion

In 1676, a group of colonists in Virginia revolted against the House of Burgesses. The basis of the rebellion is confused; many of the rebels wanted an all-out war against the local Indians, who were thought to have been stealing from the colonists. But in addition, the rebellion seems to have been fueled by economics and class resentment against the aristocracy of the colony. They demanded an end to "unjust taxes," for nepotism in government appointments, and for keeping the fur trade in the hands of the wealthy.

The rebellion didn't last long; the leader, Nathaniel Bacon, died of illness, and a British warship sent ashore some troops who quashed the uprising. But it reflects the significant class tensions within the colonies well before their rebellion against the English a hundred years later.

FRENCH WARS IN THE NEW WORLD

The Course of Imperial Conflict

Between the years 1689 and 1763, England and France were entangled in a struggle for supremacy. During this period, Massachusetts played a role in the skirmishes between England and France over dominance in North America. Each side used Native Americans and attacked each other's settlements. Many Massachusetts towns were destroyed, and many ships sunk; thousands of colonists were captured and killed.

KING WILLIAM'S WAR

King William's War broke out in 1689 after England's William III entered the War of the League of Augsburg against France. Native Americans, provoked by the French to attack, ravaged the English settlements in New England and New York. Retaliating, New Englanders gained control of Port Royal, a key French post in Nova Scotia. Bloody border skirmishes ensued for at least six years until the Treaty of Ryswick in 1697 halted both sides, restoring Port Royal to the French. However, this war accomplished nothing, for the treaty merely declared that the prewar positions would remain. As a result, the unresolved tensions led to further fighting.

QUEEN ANNE'S WAR

Queen Anne's War broke out in 1701. English colonists captured and burned Saint Augustine, Florida (then Spanish territory). There were massacres at the hands of French troops and their Native American allies in the colonies, and troops also tried again to wrest away control of Port Royal. The British and colonists conquered Acadia in 1710, but failed to encroach on Quebec and Montreal. When the Treaty of Utrecht ended Queen Anne's War in 1713, it ceded Acadia, as well as Newfoundland and the Hudson Bay territory, to the British. Cape Breton Island stayed French.

Champlain's Map

Samuel de Champlain produced the first accurate chart of the Atlantic coast, from Newfoundland to Cape Cod, as well as maps of the St. Lawrence valley and the Great Lakes. Champlain also created a trading post in what is now Quebec City, and established the commercial and military alliances that endured to the end of the French regime in Canada.

KING GEORGE'S WAR

King George's War broke out in 1744. The French captured and destroyed a British fort at Canso, Nova Scotia, and they took prisoners to their fortress at Cape Breton Island. Fearing the French, the governor of Massachusetts enlisted further colonial aid. Thus a militia of 4,000 sailed in British ships and fought under the command of Sir William Pepperell, a Maine merchant. They took Louisburg from the French, who reclaimed it the next year. This war ended in 1748 with the Treaty of Aix-la-Chapelle.

THE FRENCH AND INDIAN WAR

The French and Indian War (also called the Seven Years' War) finally decided the question of colonial control. It broke out in 1754 and lasted until 1763. In fact, all these early conflicts are sometimes collectively called the French and Indian Wars.

Both Britain and France had built new frontier fortresses in the Ohio Valley. English traders had forged relationships with the tribes that had previously traded solely with the French. France concluded that it had better protect its own strategic interests with a series of forts from Lake Erie to present-day Pittsburgh.

Virginia's governor tried unsuccessfully to warn the French to get out of British territory. To get the message across, he dispatched an armed force under the command of George Washington to drive off the French. But the French had a surprise for Washington. They defeated his troops at the Battle of Fort Necessity in 1754, sending them back to Virginia. This officially started the French and Indian War.

The End of French Power

The Treaty of Paris in 1763 ended more than a century and a half of French power in the New World. French control of Canada went to Britain, and France ceded all of its territories east of the Mississippi River to the British as well. Spain also gave Florida to the British.

The following year, British general Edward Braddock with British regulars and colonial troops attempted to take Fort Duquesne (now Pittsburgh), but the French and Native Americans prevailed. There were some sporadic British victories. However, the French and Native Americans won battle after battle—at least until 1758, when British and colonial troops seized Louisburg as well as Forts Duquesne, Frontenac, and Ticonderoga. The British also claimed Fort Niagara, and that left French Canada open to attack.

In winning this war, though, Britain doubled its national debt and took on more territory than it could easily manage. The British tried to compel colonists to pay for these campaigns against French Canada, which did not sit well with the American colonies.

TOBACCO AND COTTON

Economic Pillars of the Colonies

Two crops largely determined the development of the Southern colonies' economy: tobacco and cotton. Of the two, tobacco was initially the most important. Gradually, however, it was replaced by cotton until by the middle of the nineteenth century, cotton was king. So important and massive was the cotton crop that Southern politicians believed they could easily win the Civil War by convincing European powers (particularly Great Britain) to support their cause since Southern cotton was essential to the economic health of Europe.

TOBACCO

The European discovery of tobacco dates back to Columbus, who was offered dried tobacco leaves as a gift by one of the Native Americans he encountered on his first voyage. The Indians smoked it or chewed its leaves both for the narcotic effect and for medicinal reasons. By the 1530s, tobacco use was spreading in Europe.

Walter Raleigh and Tobacco

Sir Walter Raleigh is sometimes credited with introducing tobacco to Europe. This is incorrect; he was the first to bring Virginia tobacco across the Atlantic, but a Spaniard, Rodrigo de Jerez, one of Columbus's crew members, had demonstrated smoking on his return to Spain.

Not everyone in Europe was enthusiastic about the new substance; clergymen preached against it, and King James I of England and Scotland wrote a pamphlet denouncing its use. However, it spread with astonishing rapidity, not only in Europe but through the Middle East and Asia. The sultan of the Ottoman Empire banned its use in the seventeenth century, but his successor, with an eye toward the empire's coffers, lifted the ban and merely taxed it.

In the colonies, tobacco became so important to the economy that for a time in Virginia and Maryland it became legal currency and could be used to purchase food.

COTTON

Although cotton had been cultivated for many centuries, its importance increased dramatically with the onset of the Industrial Revolution in Europe during the eighteenth century. Beginning in 1730, cotton was spun by machines, leading to a spiraling demand for the raw product from the Americas. Climate conditions in the Southern colonies, as well as an abundance of fertile land, favored cotton as an important crop, and southern planters imported slave labor to harvest it. Thus the tragedy of slavery and the ensuing Civil War was born from the scientific breakthroughs of the Industrial Revolution.

TAXATION AND REPRESENTATION

The Road to Revolution

In many respects, the French and Indian War set the stage for the American Revolution. Britain had been engaged in the Seven Years' War in Europe, of which the American conflict had been only a part. The British treasury had to be replenished, as the war efforts had nearly doubled the national debt. King George III, now the monarch of all North American lands east of the Mississippi, tried to tighten his rein on the colonies. This vast kingdom would require not only further sources of revenue but additional administration, or so the king thought.

One of King George's edicts was the Proclamation of 1763, whereby the king established a boundary beyond which colonists could not settle. However, this spurred many adventurous souls to further exploration and trespassing.

NO TAXATION WITHOUT REPRESENTATION

When Parliament tried to raise revenues at home, the British subjects rioted in protest of additional levies, and they succeeded in making their point. Still in need of money, the British government looked across the ocean.

Parliament levied high duties on various commodities needed in the colonies—everyday items such as molasses and sugar. Thus, the Sugar Act, passed in 1764, became the first significant tax demanded of colonists. Furthermore, Parliament passed the Currency Act, whereby the colonies could not issue their own money. All transactions had to be made with gold. This angered the independent-minded colonists, who did not want to be financially dependent on England.

In addition, Parliament decided to enforce a previous law that had been passed in the 1650s but largely ignored. The Navigation Act of 1651 stipulated that goods imported or exported by British colonies (including those in Africa, Asia, or America) had to be shipped on vessels constructed by British shipbuilders. The crews sailing these vessels also had to have 75 percent British crewmen. Goods from the colonies also had to arrive on British ships. Another Navigation Act of 1660 stated that the colonists could ship particular items such as tobacco, rice, and indigo only to another British colony or to the mother country. That meant the colonists were not permitted to trade with other countries. Further laws prevented the manufacture of products such as hats and iron in the colonies, for it was thought industry in America would threaten England's economic health.

New England town meetings were still common in the 1760s, and it was at one of these that the colonists bonded around the famous slogan "No taxation without representation." When the New Englanders protested peacefully with a boycott of English goods, Parliament took little notice. Shortly thereafter, the Quartering Act of 1765 declared that colonial citizens would have to provide food and housing for royal troops, a decree that understandably cast a financial hardship on the colonials as well as a blatant invasion of their privacy.

THE STAMP ACT

The worst was yet to come as the British Parliament began to tax even more products. The Stamp Act required colonists to pay extra for newspapers, land deeds, dice, and card games—even graduation diplomas, since every paper document would require a revenue stamp from a British agent. This further infuriated the colonists, who earnestly held to the belief that these taxes were the result of their lack of representation in the British Parliament. Interestingly enough, Prime Minister Grenville had given the colonies an opportunity to avert Parliament's stamp tax and create a tax of their own to meet the costs of maintaining troops in the colonies. The colonists did not take advantage of this opportunity.

An Internal Tax

Prior to the enactment of the Grenville Program in 1765, the Crown's taxes on the colonists had been external—in other words, taxes on commerce that America engaged in with the rest of the world, i.e., tariffs. The Stamp Act, passed on March 22, 1765, was the first internal tax, a tax on activities of the colonists within their own localities.

The dissenters succeeded in getting the measure repealed, but the victory was bittersweet. The next edict—the Declaratory Act—stated that the British Parliament could create laws for the colonies however it saw fit. The Townshend Acts levied tariffs on imports such as glass, lead, paint, and tea. The colonies continued to protest, and in April 1770, Parliament repealed the Townshend taxes, except for the levy on tea.

REBELS AMONG US

Opposing the Stamp Act, the Sons of Liberty soon organized with leaders such as Samuel Adams, John Hancock, and Paul Revere. This secret, patriotic society kept meeting after the act was repealed in 1766, forming the Committees of Correspondence that fostered resistance to British economic control. The Sons of Liberty also defied the British dictates by helping American merchants who refused to import goods carried in British ships.

Educated at Harvard, Samuel Adams was a law student and merchant. But when his own ventures failed, he joined his father in a brewery business. But Adams was known for his rebellious posture against many of the British acts. Active in Boston political circles, he was elected to the lower house of the General Court and promoted the Boston chapter of the Sons of Liberty.

Paul Revere, a silversmith and engraver, was also a patriot. His elegant silverware, bowls, pitchers, and tea sets were favorites of Boston aristocracy, but he also used his talents to make artificial teeth, surgical instruments, and engraved printing plates.

Patrick Henry was a self-educated statesman who rose to prominence in the colonies as a lawyer and later as a member of the Virginia legislature, the House of Burgesses, where he introduced resolutions against the Stamp Act.

John Hancock was another Harvard-educated patriot who became a wealthy colonial businessman after inheriting his mercantile firm. Elected to the Massachusetts legislature, Hancock was soon at odds with the British government in 1768 when customs officials seized his sloop after he failed to pay import duties on his cargo. His zealous defense won him popularity among people opposed to British control of the colonies.

All of these men would play integral roles in the unfolding of the future political drama.

THE BOSTON MASSACRE

On March 5, 1770, a group of colonists living in Boston were demonstrating in front of the not-too-popular Customs House, where British troops had been called to quell the American protests. The colonists felt beleaguered, and there were harsh words and bitter tensions. The squad of soldiers responded by firing shots into the crowd, killing five people. Crispus Attucks became the first to die for American liberty. Attucks was of mixed descent, most likely a man of black, white, and Native American heritage. The event became known as the Boston Massacre, depicted by Paul Revere in one of his most famous engravings.

Paul Revere Propaganda

Paul Revere's engraving of the Boston Massacre is a good example of colonial propaganda. Revere shows the British soldiers standing in a straight line and firing point-blank into a mostly unarmed, defenseless group of colonists. Most eyewitness accounts did not agree with Revere's depiction of the event.

The Boston Massacre, though a tragic brawl, was probably not as heroic as the patriots depicted it. Nonetheless, it stirred passions for personal liberty, justice, and independence.

TEA, ANYONE?

After the repeal of the Townshend Acts, the tea tax was the only remaining tariff. Even though Parliament awarded a monopoly on the sale of tea to Britain's primary tea producer, the East India Company, which sold tea directly at lower prices than the colonial middlemen could offer, the issue of taxation stung.

Sipping a little less tea was a small annoyance made into a mountain of resentment because of the tax. When half a million pounds of tea was sent to the four primary ports—Philadelphia, New York, Charleston, and Boston—anti-British sentiment rallied to the point that tea-laden ships turned back from Philadelphia and New York, unable to unload. That left Boston, where the governor was adamant that colonists pay the levy. In December 1773, as the loaded ships sat at anchor, Samuel Adams, Paul Revere, and more than 100 patriots (some dressed as Native Americans) boarded the ships and dumped some 340 chests of tea into Boston Harbor. This bold act, known as the Boston Tea Party, met with the king's wrath; in response, he closed the port of Boston and imposed a military government.

These restrictions, known as Intolerable Acts, were meant to punish the citizens of Massachusetts for their rebellious attitude. It didn't take long for the other colonies to surmise that their liberty also might be at stake.

LEXINGTON AND CONCORD

The Shot Heard 'Round the World

The cockpit of the struggle between Crown and colonies was Massachusetts. In September 1774, General Thomas Gage sent troops to seize some cannon and powder stockpiled in Cambridge and Charleston. The Massachusetts Assembly responded by meeting in defiance of Gage's orders and reconstituted itself as the Provincial Congress. It appointed John Hancock to the head of a Committee of Safety, charged with supervising the colony's defenses. Alarmed, Gage began fortifying Boston Neck, the narrow strip of land that connected the town to the mainland.

THE MINUTEMEN

To ensure its control over the militia, the Provincial Congress asked for the resignation of all its officers. Only politically reliable men were reappointed. Select companies of the militia were formed to deal with emergencies, and to be "ready at a minute's warning with arms and ammunition."

Across the colony, men began drilling. The Provincial Congress also began collecting military equipment at Concord. Among the supplies gathered there were 20,000 pounds of cartridges and musket balls.

THE BRITISH PLAN

General Gage in Boston was anxious to disrupt the Provincial Congress's military preparations. He sent a force to Salem to confiscate some supplies stored there, but his troops turned back in the face of an ominous gathering of Minutemen. For all his well-armed and disciplined soldiers, Gage was a prisoner behind his fortified lines at Boston.

On April 14, Gage received orders from Lord Dartmouth, the colonial secretary, to take action to restore Royal authority in Massachusetts. Dartmouth wrote that "force should be repelled by force." London had decided that its laws must be enforced, even at the risk of war. In a conversation with Thomas Hutchinson, the former governor of Massachusetts, Lord North made it clear that "for aught he could see it must come to violence." Gage decided to strike the arms depot at Concord. He wanted to capture the munitions and the patriot leaders Samuel Adams and John Hancock who were staying in nearby Lexington.

LEXINGTON AND CONCORD

Gage wanted his raid to be a secret. Unfortunately for the British, they were surrounded by watchful eyes, and the expedition became common knowledge in Boston. On the night of April 18–19, the Patriot leader Joseph Warren sent Paul Revere and William Dawes riding into the country to give warning of the British movement. Along the way, they were joined by Samuel Prescott. Dodging among British patrols, the three men roused the Minutemen. That evening the British column of around 700 men under Lieutenant Colonel

Francis Smith and Major John Pitcairn set out for Concord. As they marched along they detained anyone they met to maintain secrecy, but all around their route armed men were hurrying to muster points.

FIRST SHOTS AT LEXINGTON

The road to Concord ran through Lexington. Seventy Minutemen gathered there under the command of Captain John Parker. For warmth they huddled in a tavern and some nearby homes. When word came that the British were arriving, they lined up on the village green. Parker told his men, "Stand your guard. Don't fire unless fired upon. But if they mean to have a war, let it begin here."

By the rude bridge that arched the flood,
Their flag to April's breeze unfurled.
Here once the embattled farmers stood
And fired the shot heard round the world.
—*Ralph Waldo Emerson*, "Concord Hymn"

Major Pitcairn commanded the British vanguard. Seeing the militia, he deployed his men. Then he rode toward the Americans and shouted, "Lay down your arms, you damned rebels, and disperse." The Minutemen, hopelessly outnumbered, were ordered by Parker to retreat. They began to back away but did not drop their weapons. "Lay down your arms! Damn you! Why don't you lay down your arms?" cried Pitcairn. At this point, someone, no one knows whom, fired a shot. The British volleyed into the Americans twice and charged. Able to get off only a few ragged shots, the Americans were driven off, leaving behind eight dead and ten wounded.

THE BATTLE OF CONCORD

The British pressed on to Concord. They found that Adams and Hancock had slipped away, and most of the supplies had been removed and hidden. They could do little damage. In the meantime, large numbers of angry militiamen were gathering. At the North Bridge a number of these men moved forward and opened fire, killing or wounding fourteen men. Lieutenant Colonel Smith ordered his men to retreat. As the British column began the sixteen-mile march back to Boston, bands of militia began to attack from every direction. As more and more of the exposed redcoats fell, unit cohesion began to fail, and the column degenerated into a panic-stricken mob. Only the timely arrival at Lexington of 1,000 reinforcements under Brigadier General Earl Percy saved Smith's force from destruction.

After an hour's rest, the British column moved on, with Smith's men sheltered by Percy's. Americans continued to set ambushes for the exhausted redcoats. Enraged British troops entered any house from which they believed they were sniped. Flanking parties of light troops hunted unwary Minutemen. The sight of burning homes along the roadway in turn infuriated the growing militia. Had the Americans enjoyed a unified command, the British column probably never would have limped into the shelter of Boston. As it was, British casualties totaled roughly 270 killed, 174 wounded, and twenty-six missing. The Americans had also suffered, but not as heavily—ninety-five were dead, wounded, or missing.

The bloodshed at Lexington and Concord marked the ultimate failure of British policy in America. The king, his ministers, and Parliament had repeatedly misunderstood and underestimated the colonists. Frustrated, they had willfully—even recklessly—launched a war that would spin out of their control.

THE DECLARATION OF INDEPENDENCE

Voice of a New People

Sentiment for independence gradually grew in 1776. At the opening of the war, only a few Americans, such as the Adams cousins, John and Sam, believed that the colonies must separate themselves from Britain. Most clung to the belief that the American resolution demonstrated at Boston and elsewhere would persuade the authorities in London to change course. The Americans were aware that they had friends in Parliament, like the eloquent Edmund Burke, and potential allies among British merchants, who would not like the lucrative American trade disrupted. The Olive Branch Petition sent by Congress to the king embodied these hopes. Most Americans would have been happy with a political solution that guaranteed American rights and self-government within the framework of the British Empire.

A HARDENING OF ATTITUDES

The British government's rejection of compromise shook American attachment to the empire. The motions of men like Burke were defeated by large margins in Parliament. Petitions urging peace circulated by associations of merchants were disregarded. In a message to Parliament, George III denounced the "authors and promoters of this desperate conspiracy.... They meant only to amuse, by vague expressions of attachment to the Parent State, and the strongest pro-testations of loyalty to me, whilst they were preparing for a general revolt. . . . The rebellious war now levied . . . is manifestly carried on for the purpose of establishing an independent empire." The gulf in sentiment between the Americans and their mother country had never been more manifest.

The Prohibitory Act inflicted more concrete harm. By cutting off its trade, the British government threatened America with economic ruin. John Adams pointed out that the Prohibitory Act "makes us independent in spite of our supplications and entreaties." The Brit-ish government dealt another devastating psychological blow to fraying loyalties when it began hiring German mercenaries for the war. To a people instructed by seventeenth-century English history that standing armies were instruments of oppression, the king and Parliament confirmed their tyrannical intent by unleashing foreign mercenaries on them. For a growing number of people in the colo-nies, the customary ties to Britain were increasingly meaningless. The British themselves were making it clear that American liberties would never be safe within the empire.

A REMARKABLE PAMPHLET

In January 1776, Thomas Paine, a journalist working in Philadelphia, published a brief argument for independence. He called it *Common Sense*. Plainspoken and passionate, Paine brilliantly made the case for separation from Britain. He provided his less articulate country-men a rationale for a step that they had been inching toward. More than 100,000 copies of *Common Sense* were printed in 1776—a number astonishing by the standards of the eighteenth century. The rapid dissemination of Paine's pamphlet throughout the colonies was a remarkable intellectual and political phenomenon.

THOMAS PAINE

Thomas Paine was born in England. After working unsuccessfully as a tax officer, Paine met Benjamin Franklin, who helped him move to Philadelphia in 1774. In America, Paine found work on a newspaper and embraced the cause of American independence.

Paine's rhetorical strategy was to cut to the heart of the dispute between the colonies and their mother country. He did not devote a lot of space to addressing the crisis over taxation. Paine believed the issues that had led to the war were merely symptomatic. He argued that the real problem was Britain's monarchical system. Paine directly attacked George III, calling the king a "Royal Brute." He could be nothing less, since the enlightened despots of the day were the heirs of tyrants who had seized power by force, "the first of them nothing better than the principal ruffian of some restless gang."

Paine questioned the legitimacy of monarchy, writing in words that resonated with Americans: "For all men being originally equals, no *one* by *birth* could have a right to set up his own family in perpetual preference to all others for ever." Thus the British government was by definition "rotten." That is why the mother country could oppress its colonies with corrupt laws, and when they resisted, attack them with armies of hirelings. Paine accepted American exceptionalism. America's mission was to be the last refuge of liberty. He called America "an asylum for mankind." Paine concluded that Americans must divorce themselves from the wickedness of Britain: "The blood of the slain, the weeping voice of nature cries, 'TIS TIME TO PART.'"

Paine's denunciation of monarchy and call for a republic that enshrined human liberty was profoundly compelling to his contemporaries. George Washington paid tribute to the "sound doctrine and unanswerable reasoning" of *Common Sense*. Paine popularized the idea of independence; he helped give the movement toward separation from Britain irresistible momentum.

THE DEBATE IN CONGRESS

The sentiment for independence gained ground early in 1776. By the spring, various provincial assemblies were ready to authorize their delegates in Congress to vote for independence. Generally, representatives from those colonies that had seen fighting—New England and the south—were more ready to embrace such a measure than those from middle colonies like Pennsylvania and New York, which had been more peaceful. In the end, the impetus for independence could not be denied. The wounds of a year of war, the continuing hostility of the British government, tangibly expressed in a gathering armament under General Howe, and the eloquence of advocates such as Paine could not be answered by any countervailing arguments. Opponents of independence could plausibly point out the dangers of separating from Britain; what they could not do was demonstrate how American rights could ever be safe again under British rule.

A RESOLUTION FOR INDEPENDENCE

As early as January, the Massachusetts delegation received instructions that opened up the possibility of supporting independence.

Similar freedom was given to the South Carolina delegation in March and the Georgia delegation in April. A loyalist uprising in North Carolina and the British military's depredations in Virginia led the patriots in these colonies to demand separation from Britain as well. On April 12, North Carolina became the first colony to give its congressional delegation permission to vote for independence. Virginia went even further. On May 15, the Virginia delegation to Congress was told to propose American independence.

Formation of States

With independence, the colonies began to regard themselves in new ways. No longer dependencies of Great Britain, they began calling themselves states. The challenge of the future would be to work out their relationships with each other and a new central authority.

Richard Henry Lee obeyed these instructions on June 7. He submitted a resolution that read, "Resolved: That these United Colonies are, and of right ought to be, free and independent states; that they are absolved from all allegiance to the British Crown, and that all political connection between them and the State of Great Britain is, and ought to be, totally dissolved." Lee also called for a confederation of the colonies and for a diplomatic effort to find allies in Europe. Implicit in Lee's resolutions was a recognition that Americans would carry on the war, not as rebels against their lawful sovereign, but as citizens of a confederation threatened by aggression.

This was truly revolution. Not only was Lee demanding the end of a time-honored imperial relationship with Britain and the creation of new "Continental" governmental institutions, but he was asking of Americans an existential revolution that would reshape how they understood themselves. Here was tacit acknowledgement of John Adams's point that the revolution was effected in people's hearts and minds before it was won on the battlefield.

ARGUMENTS PRO AND CON

Congress vigorously debated the resolution for independence. Distinguished men opposed the resolution, among them John Dickinson, Robert Morris, and James Wilson of Pennsylvania and James Duane of New York. John Dickinson, who had won fame as the author of *Letters from a Farmer in Pennsylvania: To the Inhabitants of the British Colonies*, argued most passionately against independence. He still hoped for the possibility of reconciliation with Britain and feared the escalating effect a declaration of independence would have on the war. He wanted a limited war for limited objectives. Dickinson was wise enough to recognize that the revolution and its war were escaping the control of cautious men like him and courageous enough to defend his principles in a losing battle. He acknowledged to his fellow congressmen, "My conduct this day I expect will give the finishing blow to my . . . popularity. Yet I had rather forfeit popularity forever, than vote away the blood and happiness of my countrymen."

Dickinson argued that independence would alienate America's friends in Britain. It would also intensify the divisions among Americans. He did not believe the colonies were prepared to fight the all-out war with Britain that would ensue if independence was declared. Britain was the greatest military power in the world. Such a war would destroy the towns and cities of the colonies. All would be ruined. If the Americans were able to protract their resistance, they and their British opponents would be so weakened that the predatory French and Spanish would sweep in and subject the colonies to their rule.

Ringing the Liberty Bell

The Liberty Bell was first hung in the State House in Philadelphia in 1753. It was rung at the opening of the First Continental Congress and after Lexington and Concord. In 1777, all of the bells in Philadelphia were hidden so the British could not melt them down for cannon. The Liberty Bell was restored to the State House in 1778.

The proponents of independence pointed out that the actions of the British government ruled out reconciliation on Dickinson's terms. The king and Parliament were determined to crush American resistance. Under such circumstances, independence and confederation offered the best hope of maintaining American unity in the face of this threat.

As Benjamin Franklin memorably put it, "We must all hang together, or, assuredly, we shall all hang separately." No one could deny the dangers America faced from the British. One of the best ways to counter British power would be to court the French and Spanish governments that Dickinson feared. But rebels would never win their assistance; only representatives of a sovereign state could treat with Paris and Madrid. Finally, independence was a reality expressed by Congress itself. The colonists were already beginning to think of themselves as Americans as well as provincials. Thomas Jefferson wrote, " . . . the question was not whether, by a declaration of independence, we should make ourselves what we are not; but whether we should declare a fact which already exists."

THE DECLARATION

Congress debated independence for several days in June but put off further debate until July 1. That day the first vote on independence took place. Nine colonies supported Lee's resolution; South Carolina, Delaware, Pennsylvania, and New York held back. A few hours later the South Carolina delegation made it known that they would not stand in the way of independence.

On July 2, Caesar Rodney of Delaware arrived after an eighty-mile ride. His vote moved Delaware into the affirmative column. The abstention of Robert Morris and another colleague shifted the balance of the Pennsylvania delegation in favor of independence. When the votes were tallied, twelve colonies had voted for Lee's resolution. The New York delegation, lacking instructions from home, abstained from the vote. Five days later, they received permission to vote with the others and the vote for independence became unanimous.

John Dickinson

John Dickinson displayed nobility in defeat. Unwilling to sign the Declaration of Independence, he resigned from Congress. He joined the army as a common soldier. He was, as he wrote, still devoted to "the defense and happiness of those unkind countrymen whom I cannot forbear to esteem as fellow-citizens amidst their fury against me."

Congress rejoiced in the founding of a new nation. A delighted John Adams wrote Abigail, "The Second Day of July 1776 will be the most memorable Epocha in the history of America. I am apt to believe that it will be celebrated by succeeding generations as the great anniversary Festival. It ought to be commemorated, as the

Day of Deliverance, by Solemn Acts of Devotion to God Almighty. It ought to be solemnized with Pomp and Parade, with Shews, Games, Sports, Guns, Bells, Bonfires, and Illuminations, from one End of this Continent to the other, from this Time forward, forevermore." Adams was correct in believing that American independence would long be celebrated in the manner that he proposed. But July 2 would not be the day.

THOMAS JEFFERSON

American Renaissance Man

Thomas Jefferson's father, Colonel Peter Jefferson, was a planter and public official. Colonel Jefferson died when Thomas was just fourteen, leaving him to be the head of the family. Thomas Jefferson's mother, Jane Randolph, was a member of one of the most distinguished families in Virginia. Jefferson was a quick learner and excelled at college. His years at school and studying law prepared him for the many tasks that would be asked of him.

The Roots of Jefferson's Learning

Thomas Jefferson's father was self-taught but according to his son was so well respected that he was chosen with Joshua Fry, professor of mathematics at William and Mary, to create the definitive map of Virginia.

When Jefferson was three, his father took on the responsibility of raising the orphaned children of his friend William Randolph. Jefferson grew up with the Randolph children and his own seven siblings. He was tutored at home by a clergyman named William Douglas. After attending Reverend James Maury's school for two years, he gained entrance to the College of William and Mary. Jefferson enjoyed dancing and playing the violin along with fox hunting and shooting.

COLLEGE AND BEYOND

Jefferson thrived at college. He became close friends with three older men: Governor Francis Fauquier, William Small, and George Wythe, the first American law professor. He spent many evenings with these men in political and philosophical discussions. After graduating, he studied law for five years with George Wythe and was admitted to the Virginia bar in 1767.

MARRIAGE

Jefferson did not marry until he was twenty-nine. He had previously stated that he was not interested in marriage because, "[m]any and great are the comforts of a single state." He was known for numerous romances throughout his youth. However, he did eventually settle down with Martha Wayles Skelton.

Scandal!

In 1802, a journalist named James Callender wrote that Jefferson kept Sally Hemings as his "concubine." This rumor continued to be discussed throughout the nineteenth century. One interesting side note to the story is that Jefferson freed all of Hemings's children when they came of age. Hers was the only one of Jefferson's slave families to be freed in its entirety.

Martha was an extremely wealthy widow who doubled Jefferson's holdings. They moved into Monticello, a home Jefferson built on land that he had inherited from his father. Unfortunately, only two of their six children lived to maturity: Martha "Patsy" and Mary "Polly."

When Jefferson's wife, Martha, died in 1782 after only ten years of marriage, he was distraught and never remarried.

Over the years, many have claimed that Thomas Jefferson had a long-standing relationship with Sally Hemings, one of his slaves. Sally was the child of a slave, Elizabeth Hemings, and Jefferson's father-in-law, John Wayles. In 1787, Sally accompanied Jefferson's daughter Mary when Mary went to Paris to join her father. Some claim this is when the relationship between Hemings and Jefferson began.

Sally had six children, and there seems to have been a window of opportunity for Jefferson to have been the father of each of them. Further, DNA tests have shown that Jefferson could have been the father of the children.

MONTICELLO

Amid the strains of his life and the tragedy of his wife's death, Jefferson found solace in the house he built on a mountain near Charlottesville, Virginia. He named it Monticello, or "Little Mountain." It became the project on which he lavished his inventiveness, his artistic sensibilities, and—unfortunately—his money for the rest of his life.

He began the house in 1768 and built continuously on it for the rest of his life. Visitors describe stepping over ditches and bending beneath scaffolding as they navigated their way through the rooms. However, the house displayed Jefferson's remarkable interests. It included, among other things:

- A bed that was built between two rooms; which room you were in depended on which side of the bed you got out on

- A massive clock over the entrance, with both exterior and interior faces
- Dumbwaiters to carry food from the kitchens
- A pond stocked with fresh fish

In 1815 Jefferson sold his library to the U.S. government to replace the national library that had been destroyed by British troops during the War of 1812. The sale was not wholly disinterested; Jefferson needed the money to pay off the debts incurred by his beloved building project.

Slave Plantation

The dark side of Monticello was that the work on it was done by slaves. Despite his ideals, expressed in the Declaration of Independence, Jefferson remained a slave owner his whole life. Slaves at Monticello were housed in separate quarters. From there they went out every day to labor in the fields or in their master's nail-making factory (a project that was an abject failure). When we say that Jefferson "built" Monticello, what we really mean is that his slaves built it for him.

JEFFERSON'S CURIOSITY

Along with Benjamin Franklin, Jefferson was perhaps the most relentlessly curious of the Founding Fathers. He read extensively about the scientific advances being made in Europe and carried out various experiments at Monticello, most of them having to do with improving growing methods. After the War of Independence, he served as Washington's secretary of state, then as the nation's third president, during which he doubled the size of the new nation through the Louisiana Purchase. But his heart remained in Monticello.

Jefferson's great passion in retirement was creating the University of Virginia. He designed the campus, hired the professors, and created the curriculum. When it opened, he became the university's first rector.

Epitaph

Jefferson's own view of his accomplishments is attested to by his epitaph, which he composed for his grave at Monticello:

Here was buried Thomas Jefferson
Author of the Declaration of American Independence
Of the Statute of Virginia for Religious Freedom
And Father of the University of Virginia

GEORGE WASHINGTON

First in the Hearts of His Countrymen

The colonies, wrapped in a crisis with Britain, sought a hero, someone who could exercise decisive leadership and find a way forward. They got George Washington, who, by his leadership of the revolutionary army, and still more through his presidency, created the American political myth of the citizen-soldier-statesman that has prevailed ever since.

Washington was born on February 22, 1732, in Westmoreland County, Virginia. His father, Augustine Washington, was a wealthy Virginia planter. Washington was born to Augustine's second wife, Mary Ball. He grew up in a relatively wealthy and comfortable environment.

Washington's mother was overprotective and demanding throughout his life. When his brother thought that service in the British Navy might suit Washington, his mother prohibited him from joining. She often demanded his attention for money and other comforts, even while he was in the midst of fighting during the Revolutionary War.

GROWING UP WITH LAWRENCE

Washington's father died when he was only eleven, and his half brother, Lawrence, took over raising him. When Washington was sixteen, he went to live with Lawrence at Mount Vernon.

He did not study in Great Britain as was normal for young men during that time. Instead, he was taught in colonial Virginia, although it is not certain where or by whom. Washington was good at math, which suited his chosen profession of surveying, an important occupation as land was claimed and developed.

The Cherry Tree Myth

Washington did not, in fact, cut down a cherry tree and then tell his father the truth. This story was an invention of author Mason Weems, who wrote a book called *The Life of Washington* shortly after Washington's death in which Weems glorified Washington and his life.

In 1749, Washington was appointed as surveyor for Culpeper County, Virginia, after a trek for Lord Fairfax into the Blue Ridge Mountains. He used the money he earned to buy land, eventually becoming one of the largest landholders in the country. He rented much of this land to tenant farmers.

Washington acquired Mount Vernon in 1754. Washington loved working the land at Mount Vernon and tried new techniques in raising livestock and agriculture. He also enjoyed the social life that being a wealthy planter afforded him.

MARTHA DANDRIDGE CUSTIS WASHINGTON

Washington got engaged to Martha Dandridge Custis in 1758. At the same time, it appears that he was in love with Sally Fairfax, his neighbor's wife, although there is no evidence that the affection was returned. However, he married Martha on January 6, 1759, and the marriage was long-lasting and happy. She had two children from a previous marriage along with a great deal of money and land.

Martha Washington

Martha Washington had to deal with much hardship following her husband through his military command and presidency, but she always maintained high spirits. In her words: "I am still determined to be cheerful and happy, in whatever situation I may be; for I have also learned from experience that the greater part of our happiness or misery depends upon our dispositions, and not upon our circumstances."

While Martha did not receive a formal education, she knew how to efficiently run a household. She was a warm hostess much admired by all. She also loved her family and her privacy; unfortunately this need for privacy led her to burn the letters she had exchanged with her husband before her own death in 1802.

MILITARY HERO AND NATIONAL LEADER

Washington began his military career in 1752 as a part of the Virginia militia. In 1753, he volunteered as a messenger to the French at Fort LeBoeuf on Lake Erie. The journey took two and a half months and was full of hardship. His message demanded that the French leave the Ohio Valley. However, the French refused, an action that led to the French and Indian War.

Washington was promoted to colonel of the Virginia troops. He felt the French would attack and built Fort Necessity to stop them, but was forced to surrender Fort Necessity to the French on July 4, 1754. He resigned from the military in 1754, but then rejoined in 1755 as an aide-de-camp to General Edward Braddock. When Braddock was killed in battle with the French forces, Washington managed to stay calm and keep the unit together as they retreated. As Washington wrote later, " . . . I had four bullets through my coat, and two horses shot under me, yet escaped unhurt, altho' death was levelling my companions on every side!"

COMMANDER IN CHIEF

Washington served in the military from 1752 to 1758 and was elected to the Virginia House of Burgesses in 1758. While serving in the House, he spoke out against Britain's policies until the House of Burgesses was disbanded in 1776.

From 1774 to 1775, he represented Virginia in both Continental Congresses. He strongly believed in the need to use military action in response to British actions restricting liberty. He was unanimously named commander-in-chief of the Continental Army. He took the position without pay, accepting only reimbursement for his expenses, which actually resulted in him making more money in the end.

Washington's challenge was not merely to create an army capable of defeating the British. He had to form this force from citizens who were not, in many cases, much inclined to obey military discipline and few of whom had any actual fighting experience. The image of colonial soldiers, each wearing a tricornered hat and with his musket held over his shoulder, marching in step down a country lane in their crisp, blue uniforms, is a product of Hollywood's wishful thinking.

Primitive Shelters

A Concord, Massachusetts, clergyman, the grandfather of the future writer Ralph Waldo Emerson, wrote of the shelters used by Washington's army: "Some are made of boards, some of sailcloth; some partially of one and partly of the other. Again, others are made of stone, or turf, brick and brush. Some are thrown up in a hurry; others are enviously wrought with doors and windows, done with wreathes and withes, in the manner of a basket."

Many of the troops lacked muskets and drilled with sticks over their shoulders. The army was perennially short of powder and other supplies; the quartermaster was corrupt, and often food intended for the troops did not reach them.

Soldiers and officers called each other by their first names, and the troops frequently disobeyed orders with which they disagreed. The wonder was not that Washington succeeded in building an army; rather it was that the raw materials he had to work with didn't run away at the first whiff of British gunpowder. His ability to forge an army that repeatedly took the field against the enemy and, on occasion, defeated it, is testimony to Washington's strength of character and his organizational skills.

BUNKER HILL TO YORKTOWN

The Course of the Revolutionary War

After the engagement at Lexington and Concord in April 1775, the British forces in Boston drew back to lick their wounds. While the leaders of the Continental Congress debated their next steps, the colonial militia in Massachusetts, on June 15, 1775, took up positions first on Bunker Hill, then on Breed's Hill overlooking Boston Harbor. The British troops attempted to dislodge them the following day, making three charges up the hill (although the battle was fought on Breed's Hill, it's been referred to as the Battle of Bunker Hill by many subsequent history books). While they succeeded eventually in forcing the colonists to retreat, the victory was a costly one for the British, who realized they were in for a long, difficult fight.

When Washington first took command, there was much strategic planning. On May 10, 1775, at the start of the Revolutionary War, Ethan Allen, an American Revolutionary soldier, led his Green Mountain Boys in an attack to overtake Fort Ticonderoga. These soldiers from Vermont seized the fort and all of its valuable artillery stores without a struggle. They then dragged fifty heavy cannons by sled from Fort Ticonderoga in northern New York to Boston. An astute Washington had the cannons mounted on Dorchester Heights, which commanded the city. British general William Howe saw this and fled by sea to Halifax, Nova Scotia, where he awaited the reinforcement of German mercenaries from Europe. This brought a much-needed reprieve from the occupation of any British troops in the colonies.

BATTLING FOR NEW YORK

Britain's clear advantage was its navy, for the Americans had none. Sensing the final break even before the Declaration of Independence was signed, in June of 1776, the British sent General Howe to assemble his forces as well as a huge fleet. Howe landed on Long Island, pushing his way to New York City with an army of 30,000 soldiers— more than twice as many men as Washington had. Trying to cope with this mighty force, Washington committed a tactical blunder that nearly cost him the war. He split his troops between Brooklyn on Long Island and Manhattan Island. This weakened the overall American position. By the end of August, the Americans had to retreat to their Brooklyn Heights fortifications.

Long Island Chowder

During the revolution, when General William Howe and his British forces occupied New York City, they placed an enormous demand on the milk and cream products coming from Long Island. Long Islanders were forced to substitute tomatoes and water broth for the cream in their chowder. Therefore, the proper name for red clam chowder would be Long Island clam chowder, rather than Manhattan clam chowder, as it is called.

Thinking he had them cornered, Howe called off his redcoats temporarily while he planned a potential siege. This proved to be a mistake. Surrender was not on Washington's mind. Though he had no navy to rely on, the undeterred general rounded up every seaworthy vessel he could find. In the midst of a raging storm, and a thick fog, he and his men rowed across the East River to safety in Manhattan, losing not one man in his command. But although this served as a brilliant escape, it also meant that an important American seaport, Brooklyn, had been lost to the British.

The New York fighting wasn't finished. Once again, General Howe took his time, hoping to negotiate a peace agreement. When those attempts failed, Howe landed his force at Kip's Bay, Manhattan, on September 15, accompanied by British warships cruising the East River. Washington, riding among his men, had trouble keeping the troops together. Rather than take advantage of the disarray, Howe displayed his leisurely posture, feeling perhaps a little smug that he controlled most of Manhattan.

American Arson

A few days after Howe landed in Manhattan, a mysterious fire leveled much of the town. Was it mere coincidence? Some have attributed it to a patriot arsonist, but whatever the fire's origin, it aided the American cause.

Washington's brilliance more than made up for his early strategic errors. As a good military strategist, he had the knack for learning from his blunders. He knew he couldn't battle the British if he didn't preserve his own army. Washington withdrew his troops for a while, retreating to Harlem Heights, then to White Plains. The British prevailed at a White Plains skirmish. While they allowed Washington's forces to retreat in good order, the British turned their attention south, capturing Fort Washington and Fort Lee on the New Jersey shore just days later.

Things were looking bleak for General Washington and his men. In three months, they had lost New York and Long Island, and his army of some 19,000 was reduced to fewer than 3,500. Desertion among the troops was rampant, and Washington was facing criticism for his performance. The circumstances became so grim that General Howe declared victory. Even the Congress fled Philadelphia for Baltimore. Such defeats inspired Thomas Paine to write in *The American Crisis*, "These are the times that try men's souls."

Washington led his contingent across the Delaware River into the relative safety of Pennsylvania. As a precaution, he ordered all boats along the New Jersey side of the river to go with them. Morale was running low as winter set in, and many troops were without proper shoes and clothing. Undeterred, Washington found his answer that frigid December.

CHRISTMAS CROSSING

When reinforcements arrived, Washington's strategic mind went to work. He knew the British had pulled back most of their troops into New York City, leaving only scattered garrisons of the mercenary Hessian soldiers. Those Hessians nearest to Washington were camped at Trenton.

Washington launched a surprise attack on the sleeping soldiers, on the morning of December 26. He was fairly certain that these foreign troops, celebrating the holidays away from home, would imbibe heavily, and that this was the optimal moment to attack. Washington gained serious ground by killing, wounding, or capturing every one of the Hessian soldiers while suffering only a small number of casualties among his men. Future American president James Monroe was one of the four wounded.

This surprise attack reminded the colonists that victory was still possible. To the British, Washington's victory proved the Continental army was worthy of their respect. British general Charles

Cornwallis rushed south from New York City toward Princeton with reinforcements. In early January, he reached Trenton, where he decided to rest.

Nathan Hale

When the British hanged Nathan Hale for being a spy on September 22, 1776, he uttered the famous line, "I only regret that I have but one life to lose for my country." His words may have been inspired by a passage from Joseph Addison's play, *Cato*: "What pity is it that we can die but once to serve our country."

Washington slipped past Trenton in the night and attacked the British the next morning. The Americans not only were victorious on the battlefield, but also were able to acquire much-needed supplies. In fact, the British felt so alarmed and threatened that they evacuated most New Jersey garrisons.

With victories in the Battle of Trenton and the Battle of Princeton, and with Philadelphia no longer in peril, Washington moved north to winter quarters in Morristown, New Jersey. There, Washington turned his attention to recruitment.

THE WAR UP NORTH

General John Burgoyne felt that by striking down the Hudson River, he would cut off New England and New York from the rest of the colonies and end the colonial rebellion. After recapturing Fort Ticonderoga, Burgoyne headed toward Fort Edward. When the patriots saw them approaching, they scattered and continued to attack from behind their shield of trees. The end result was British losses of close to 1,000 men. This slowed the British down, and by the time they reached Saratoga, New York, the Americans were ready. After losing even more soldiers, Burgoyne did what he swore he'd never do—he surrendered on October 17, 1777.

VALLEY FORGE

Trying to protect the capital of Philadelphia, Washington lost the Battles of Brandywine and Germantown, and he withdrew his besieged forces to nearby Valley Forge, the site of his winter encampment.

Although Washington held the high ground, the conditions at Valley Forge were dismal. An estimated 2,500 troops died from exposure or disease, further reducing Washington's fighting force. The men needed everything from food and soap to blankets and warm clothing. Many deserted the Continental army. Making matters worse, discontented officers tried to oust Washington and replace him with General Horatio Gates. When this attempt failed it only further solidified Washington's influence.

Spring's approach brought brighter spirits, as did the heartening news that France had allied itself with the Americans. Within six months, the Continental army was ready once more. The last major battle in the Northeast occurred at Monmouth in June 1778, when the British general Sir Henry Clinton pulled troops out of Philadelphia and moved them north toward New York. Washington's army caught up with them at Monmouth, New Jersey, where General Washington forced Clinton to retreat.

FRENCH AID

At the outset of the Revolution, Benjamin Franklin was dispatched to France to foster financial support as well as troops. Franklin's diplomatic prowess certainly succeeded, but Washington's victories spoke volumes. After seeing proof that the Continental army was a capable fighting force, and upon hearing rumors that Britain might offer America territorial concessions to reach peace, the French government ministers recommended to King Louis XVI that he sign a treaty of alliance with the Americans. In February 1778, this alliance was made formal. Soon after the signing, Spain threw in support.

French aid was certainly welcome, but French egos were not. Many of the officers who arrived in the summer of 1777 demanded exalted rank and commensurate pay for their limited military experience. An exception was the young Marquis de Lafayette, who arrived in Philadelphia volunteering to serve on America's behalf at his own expense. This quickly won Washington's praise and the admiration of American troops. In 1779, Lafayette returned to his native country to continue lobbying for further aid, thus proving to be a valuable liaison between the Continental army and the French government.

THE WAR IN THE WEST AND SOUTH

American frontiersmen continued to settle and their numbers in the region grew. This was significant because Britain had forbidden the American colonists to move beyond the Appalachians. In fact, Great Britain had recruited Native Americans as allies to attack any western colonial settlements. But George Rogers Clark, a Virginian, seized British forts along the frontier in 1778 and braved the Ohio River. By spring 1779 he arrived in the Illinois territory.

Major Battles of the Revolutionary War

- Bunker Hill/Breed's Hill (1775)
- Trenton and Princeton (1776–1777)
- Saratoga (1777)
- Charleston (1780)
- Camden (1780)
- Cowpens (1781)
- Yorktown (1781)

In the autumn of 1778, a large British force sailed from New York to launch a sea assault against Savannah, Georgia. The city fell to the British in December. Augusta, Georgia, fell one month later. When the French joined forces to counter the assault, they were shot to tatters. By the end of 1779, most of Georgia was firmly under British and Loyalist control.

While Charleston, South Carolina, had fended off attack for nearly three years, the city's defenses slowly deteriorated. The British besieged Charleston, cutting off supplies, and in May, the Americans were forced to surrender. The patriots lost many military supplies in the process.

THE WAR AT SEA

Great Britain, the world's leading maritime power, hardly feared the infant colonial navy. The British ships plied coastal waters, supplying the redcoats with whatever was needed, including more of His

Majesty's troops. Still, the small patriot navy won a few surprising victories, such as when a small American squadron captured the port of Nassau in the Bahamas.

John Paul Jones

John Paul Jones is by far the most famous Revolutionary naval hero. In 1778, Jones raided the port of Whitehaven in England and then captured the British sloop called the *Drake*. On September 23, 1779, when the British attacked his converted merchant ship the *Bonhomme Richard* and demanded his surrender, Jones answered with the famous words, "I have not yet begun to fight!"

By 1781 there were more than 450 privately owned vessels that had received commissions to attack British shipping. Although these did not impede the British troops and their supply provisions, they added tremendous cost to the war Britain waged.

Thanks to the French navy, Britain's supremacy was sufficiently threatened, and the war at sea saw fewer American defeats with added victories. French naval forces fought off the Virginia coast, successfully trapping the British general Cornwallis and his army.

The Earliest Submarine

The American *Turtle* submarine was launched in the dark of night on September 6–7, 1776, against the British flagship, HMS *Eagle*, which was moored in New York harbor. The submarine crew attempted to attach a bomb to the rudder of the British ship. While the *Turtle* failed to destroy its target, the British recognized the threat and moved the fleet.

THE BATTLE OF YORKTOWN

In 1781, Washington coordinated the land and sea operation that brought the final climax of the war. It was as if the commander had been waiting for this very moment to unleash his most brilliant military strategies and fighting energy.

First, a French fleet blockaded Yorktown early that September, followed by a combined Franco-American army that Washington commanded. It took up siege positions on land and by early October had trapped the British against the York River. In a gross misjudgment, the British commander, Lord Cornwallis, had his back to the sea. Daily he endured gunfire and continual pounding from the cannons until he was forced to ask the Americans for terms of surrender on October 17, 1781. Two days later the once mighty (and haughty) British army paraded its units between the victorious French and American soldiers, laying down their arms, while a British band played the popular tune "The World Turned Upside Down."

Unable to concede the war, Cornwallis sent a representative, General O'Hara, to surrender his sword. General O'Hara approached a French commander, who indicated that the sword should go to General Washington. However, Washington felt that an officer of equal rank should receive it. Thus, his second-in-command, Major General Benjamin Lincoln, received the British sword in surrender.

Back in England, King George III was prepared to fight on, but the British Parliament put an end to that notion. It had taken more than six years of war, and skirmishes before that, to drive its greatest overseas possession toward independence. In February 1782, Lord North's ministry in Britain fell. Parliament would no longer support a war in America.

THE CONSTITUTIONAL CONVENTION

Miracle in Philadelphia

Negotiation of the formal end of the war took five months, and the Treaty of Paris was formally signed in September 1783. Several months later Washington took leave of his army and declared his intention to return to his estate in Mount Vernon, Virginia. However, he was soon to be called back to public service.

BUILDING A NEW SYSTEM OF GOVERNMENT

The Articles of Confederation, which governed the United States during and immediately after the war, were simple. They were too limited to guide the new nation down its fought-for path of independence. There was no governor, no chief executive, and no national court to interpret the law. Each state had one vote, regardless of its population. The Congress had military and diplomatic power but could not levy taxes to pay for any of it. It couldn't regulate commerce. Any shift in power, or any change at all, required unanimous consent of the states.

The weakness of the national government reflected fear of a monarchy. George Washington saw this as a sign of weakness and disorganization. In 1785 he wrote, "...the Confederation appears to me to be little more than a shadow without the substance…" When a group of debt-ridden farmers led an insurrection against Massachusetts (called Shays' Rebellion), Washington grew alarmed and feared that the eight years of bloodshed and expense invested in the United States would be wasted unless some better structure was brought forth.

THE CONSTITUTIONAL CONVENTION

Delegates from all states, with the exception of Rhode Island, converged on Philadelphia in May 1787 to revise the Articles of Confederation. The legislature unanimously chose Washington as president of the convention, and most agreed on a few prevailing principles once Alexander Hamilton convinced the crowd that the Articles had best be scrapped and another document created.

ORIGINAL THIRTEEN STATES	
STATE	DATE ADMITTED
Delaware	December 7, 1787
Pennsylvania	December 12, 1787
New Jersey	December 18, 1787
Georgia	January 2, 1788
Connecticut	January 9, 1788
Massachusetts	February 6, 1788
Maryland	April 28, 1788
South Carolina	May 23, 1788
New Hampshire	June 21, 1788
Virginia	June 25, 1788
New York	July 26, 1788
North Carolina	November 21, 1789
Rhode Island	May 29, 1790

George Washington led the delegates, which included Benjamin Franklin, Alexander Hamilton, and James Madison. In Europe on diplomatic matters, Thomas Jefferson and John Adams missed the work and the rancor. Patrick Henry, who supported the limited central government of the Confederation, refused to attend.

Slaves and the Constitution

Moral arguments over the practice of slavery entered into the convention's debate. The delegates compromised, and the Constitution permitted slaves to be imported until 1808, when Congress could ban slave importation and trade. Northerners reluctantly agreed to the Fugitive Slave Clause that allowed owners to reclaim runaway slaves who fled to other states. Delegates also compromised on how to count slaves for purposes of population; a slave would be regarded as three-fifths of a person.

James Madison, representing Virginia, presented his alternative for a national republic with a powerful central government, which limited the sovereignty of individual states. Madison's Virginia Plan drew its authority not from the thirteen states but from the population as a whole. The convention voted to accept the Virginia Plan, with its idea of a lower house based on population, and left a committee to work out the composition of the upper house. On July 16, 1787, the committee proposed the "Great Compromise" that each state have two members in this upper house of legislative government. As part of this concept, there was a three-part national government with lower and upper houses in the legislative branch, an executive branch, and a judiciary branch.

EARLY COMPROMISES

While the delegates agreed to the basic principles that Madison and his Virginia Plan outlined early in June, they began to address contentious topics, including this issue of population in regard to representation, as well as regional issues such as slavery.

The Constitution required more work when it came to defining judicial power. The delegates created a Supreme Court and left the rest of the planning to the first Congress, which then had to tackle how this court system would be established.

They agreed that the Senate would be the governmental body filled with two delegates from each state, and that the House of Representatives would be based on population in those states. In addition, rather than have the people vote for the president and vice president, they would select members of a small Electoral College to do so. In the event that one candidate did not receive a majority of votes cast by this Electoral College, the House of Representatives was charged with making the selection.

The Original of the Constitution

The entire Constitution is displayed at the National Archives in Washington, D.C., only once a year on September 17, the anniversary of the date on which it was signed. On other days, the first and fourth pages are displayed in a bulletproof case. At night they are lowered into a vault strong enough to withstand a nuclear explosion!

The executive office would be responsible for carrying out all laws, and the executive officer, the president, would serve as commander in chief of the armed forces. It is interesting that the Founding Fathers chose to have a civilian (the president) be the chief commander of the armed forces. In addition, the president would oversee foreign relations and appoint federal judges and other federal officials.

The delegates gave the power of currency issue to the new national government. This took away from the individual states the right to issue money. The power of taxation was given to both the national and the state governments.

CHECKS, BALANCES, AND EVERYONE'S BLESSING

Delegates to the Constitutional Convention set up a system of checks and balances. For instance, even though the president also served as the commander in chief, only Congress could declare war. The delegates gave the president veto power over Congress, although with a two-thirds majority, the Congress could override such an action. The judicial checks were less thought-out at this juncture, but years later, when the chief justice of the United States declared a law unconstitutional, the judicial review process became more firmly established.

On September 17, 1787, after much debate, the convention completed the Constitution of the United States. Now, the conventioneers had to gather the delegates' formal signatures, and the states had to ratify the new document outlining the new form of government. Actually, nine states had to ratify the Constitution before it would take effect. Five states—Delaware, Pennsylvania, New Jersey, Georgia, and Connecticut—were the first to approve, and New Hampshire provided the decisive ratification vote in 1788. Some states, including New York and Pennsylvania, insisted more work be done to safeguard fundamental individual rights. Congress submitted twelve amendments, ten of which were adopted as Articles I through X of the U.S. Constitution—collectively known as the Bill of Rights. When Congress introduced the Bill of Rights in 1789, North Carolina and Rhode Island gave their formal approval to the Constitution, which was by now already operating as the law of the land.

Civil Liberties

Civil rights guaranteed under the Bill of Rights include:

- Freedom of the press
- Freedom of speech
- Freedom to assemble
- Freedom of religion
- The right to bear arms
- The right to a speedy trial
- Guarantee against cruel or unusual punishment
- The right to due process

The Preamble of the U.S. Constitution reads: "We the People of the United States, in Order to form a more perfect Union, establish Justice, insure domestic Tranquility, provide for the common defence, promote the general Welfare, and secure the Blessings of Liberty to ourselves and our Posterity, do ordain and establish this Constitution for the United States of America."

FEDERALISTS AND ANTIFEDERALISTS

Party Conflicts in the New Nation

Once the delegates signed the Constitution, they returned to their respective states and set forth to see it ratified. But two factions had different notions. Federalists believed in a strong central government; merchants and professionals made up this faction. The opposing party, the Antifederalists, was composed of mainly farmers, many of whom owed large debts. Antifederalists were alarmed that the Constitution might nullify the independence of the states. They argued that too many differing agendas in large states would make it impossible for one way to prevail.

But the Federalists accomplished a lot. They organized the administrative detail of the national government, began the liberal interpretations of the Constitution, and kept the new nation at peace with a stance of neutrality. *The Federalist Papers*, a series of newspaper articles written by Alexander Hamilton, James Madison, and John Jay, defended the new Constitution. James Madison effectively put to rest the Antifederalist argument, stating that its size would indeed make a central government work best (not impede its functioning) because no one special interest could gain much ground with such diversity throughout the land.

GEORGE WASHINGTON
AFTER THE WAR

Though worn out by battle, George Washington reluctantly accepted the call to become the first president of the republic, relinquishing his genteel retirement at Mount Vernon. Mindful that his leadership was sorely needed to unify the infant nation, he pressed for ratification of the Constitution, which he firmly believed was the best that could be written at the time.

On April 30, 1789, Washington took the oath of office on a balcony of Federal Hall on Wall Street, New York City. Also present were Vice President John Adams, both houses of the newly organized Congress, and an exuberant crowd of onlookers. His first inaugural address was brief and modest, containing only one suggestion to the new Congress—that its members " . . . would carefully avoid every alteration which might endanger the benefits of an United and effective Government, or which ought to await the future lessons of experience . . . "

Washington knew there was widespread support for the original amendments that made up the Bill of Rights. He supported these but also had the foresight to know that further attempts to amend the document too quickly would hinder the fledgling nation.

Washington respected the divisions of power created in the Constitution, and he spent his first days in office listening to divergent viewpoints as he organized the executive branch. Landowners tended to have more conservative views, and as George Washington was a propertied gentleman himself, he tried to recognize the more liberal outlook of farmers and artisans who made up the majority of the population.

Washington chose a balance of liberals and conservatives for his cabinet. Alexander Hamilton became secretary of the treasury and Henry Knox the first secretary of war; Edmund Randolph of Virginia was offered the post of attorney general. Washington awaited the return of Thomas Jefferson, who was the U.S. diplomatic representative to France, in order to offer him the position of secretary of state. Washington nominated John Jay of New York as chief justice of the United States.

The First Cabinet

The original cabinet, which is part of the "Unwritten Constitution," consisted of four departments: the State Department, Treasury Department, War Department, and the Office of the Attorney General. Today's cabinet consists of fifteen departments:

1. Agriculture
2. Commerce
3. Defense
4. Education
5. Energy
6. Health and Human Services
7. Homeland Security
8. Housing and Urban Development
9. Interior
10. Labor
11. State
12. Transportation
13. Treasury
14. Veterans Affairs
15. Office of the Attorney General

THE FEDERAL GOVERNMENT EXPANDS

During the first administration, the seat of government proposal was passed in July 1790 establishing Philadelphia as the capital until

1800, when a federal district on the Potomac would be established. The Bill of Rights was approved in 1791, and President Washington also signed a bill creating the first bank of the United States. The banking issue proved to be the first test of the Constitution's flexibility. Jefferson asserted that a bank bill was unconstitutional, but Hamilton insisted that a national bank was essential.

As the president celebrated his sixtieth birthday, Washington wasn't overjoyed that his two principal advisors—Jefferson and Hamilton—had fundamental differences. Each represented divergent philosophies of government. Hamilton's backers evolved into the Federalist Party, backing a strong central government. Those supporting Jefferson for the Republican Party, which later became known as the Democratic-Republican Party, held firm to the opinion that states should have the right to decide matters relating to them.

As the 1792 election drew near, Washington's close advisors unanimously agreed that times were too perilous to risk a transfer of the executive branch to anyone other than the current president. The Northern states were disagreeing with their Southern neighbors over the reapportionment of seats in the House of Representatives. Washington vetoed a plan that would have favored the North, viewing it as unconstitutional, and he grew anxious over the tendency of Northern and Southern states to part ways on political issues. Though he wanted to bid farewell to public life, Washington agreed to a second term and was the unanimous choice, along with Vice President Adams, in the 1792 election. This started the two-term tradition that would continue until the administration of Franklin Delano Roosevelt in the 1930s. The Twenty-second Amendment codified the two-term provision when it was ratified in 1951.

THE CREATION OF
WASHINGTON, D.C.

As a result of a compromise between Hamilton and Jefferson over the issue of economic policy, Hamilton agreed to support moving the capital to a more southern location, and in 1790 Congress passed an act approving the building of the capital on the shores of the Potomac River along the Virginia–Maryland border, an area that President George Washington had selected.

President John Adams was the first leader to govern from Federal City, later named Washington, D.C., in honor of our nation's first president. Today, the city of Washington exists as the District of Columbia (D.C.), the federal district of the United States, named after Christopher Columbus.

Washingtonians Had No Vote

Since the District of Columbia is a federal district and not a state, the inhabitants originally had no real local government, and they had no vote in federal elections. The ratification of the Twenty-third Amendment in 1961 gave Washington, D.C., three electoral votes, so its population could participate in the election of the president and vice president.

While the area was being surveyed, Washington and Thomas Jefferson selected French architect Pierre L'Enfant to design the city, which, at the time it was surveyed, included Georgetown (Maryland) and Alexandria (Virginia). L'Enfant's plan featured broad avenues radiating out from Capitol Hill, interrupted by a series of rectangular and circular parks, all overlaid with a perpendicular grid of streets.

The grid was then slashed with diagonal avenues named for the thirteen original states.

THE WHITE HOUSE

George Washington never lived in the White House; instead, since the capital during his first administration was in New York, he stayed in a mansion at 39 Broadway, the seat of government then known as Federal Hall.

John and Abigail Adams were the first president and first lady to enjoy the newly created presidential mansion. The White House, as it became known, was built between 1792 and 1800. Adams is reported to have written during his second night in the President's House (what would come to be known as the White House), " . . . I pray Heaven to bestow the best Blessings on this House and all that shall hereafter inhabit it. May none but honest and wise Men ever rule under this roof."

THE LOUISIANA PURCHASE

Doubling America

For most Americans in 1801, the American continent effectively ended at the Appalachian Mountains. Beyond them was a vast shadowy expanse, peopled with Indians, French settlers, and who knew what else? Some had heard of the great river called the Mississippi, which formed somewhere to the north and carried its waters down across the land, emptying them into the Gulf of Mexico far to the south. The mighty river was said to be miles wide in places, a magnificent highway for goods and travel—but out of reach of the newly formed United States.

Gradually, the fledgling republic expanded westward. Kentucky became a state in 1792, Tennessee in 1796. But even as new white settlers moved into these territories, they worried about the power of France and its new ruler, Napoleon Bonaparte.

Bonaparte's rise as First Consul and then emperor seemed to pose a growing threat to the United States. He sent French troops to the Caribbean to crush the slave revolt in Saint-Domingue led by Toussaint L'Ouverture. Surely he must be planning to send more armies to check America's westward expansion.

In fact, Napoleon's ambitions for the most part pointed east, not west. He envisioned a French empire extending over most of Europe—and for this he needed money. His thinking was also shaped by the fact that the army he had sent to conquer L'Ouverture was largely wiped out by malaria, making further expeditions to the New World unattractive.

For this reason, in 1803 envoys Robert Livingston and James Monroe were able to arrange with Napoleon's minister Talleyrand the sale of the Louisiana territory to the United States for $15 million.

A Mixed Reaction

Although President Jefferson himself, not to mention his envoys, was excited by the opportunity to purchase Louisiana, this wasn't the case with everyone. When word of the purchase got out, some attacked the idea. "We are to give money of which we have too little for land of which we already have too much," wrote one indignant commentator. The purchase treaty was approved by Congress by an overwhelming vote. Now Jefferson was faced with the task of evaluating just what it was he and the country had just bought.

LEWIS AND CLARK

To explore the new territory, Jefferson selected two men from his native state of Virginia: Meriwether Lewis and William Clark. (Lewis was a captain in the army; Clark is often designated as "Captain" Clark, but he was, in fact, a lieutenant.) On May 14, 1804, they set off to, in the words of Jefferson's instructions, "... explore the Missouri river, & such principal stream of it as by it's course & communication with the water of the Pacific Ocean ... may offer the most direct & practicable water communication across the continent, for the purposes of commerce."

The two men and their companions pushed on through lands previously unknown to people of European descent. They bartered with local Indians, who at this point saw no reason to be hostile to them. There were cultural clashes, but no actual fighting.

In 1805 they reached the Pacific in what is now Oregon. Returning east, they brought Jefferson a wealth of information about the new lands, including sample animals, maps, plants, sketches, and accounts of hazards encountered and opportunities discovered. The Louisiana Purchase turned out to be the best bargain ever made by an American government, effectively doubling the size of the country and making it, for the first time, a truly continental force.

THE WAR OF 1812

New Conflict with Britain

When James Madison took office as president in 1809, much of his presidency was filled with continued tension with foreign governments. The Non-Intercourse Act forbade trade with France and Great Britain, both of which had seized American ships as part of their conflict with each other.

By 1810, Madison realized the American trade boycott was having little effect, for both countries continued seizing American ships. U.S.–British relations worsened as a result of these maritime troubles and also because of America's expansion into British-held lands in the West, in Canada, and in Florida (Spanish-held at the time). Anti-British factions in Congress accused Britain of provoking Native American attacks on American frontier communities. In November 1811, Governor William Henry Harrison of Indiana fought the Shawnee nation with American troops at the Battle of Tippecanoe. Though the president had not authorized the use of troops, the incident roused support for military preparedness as war with Britain looked probable.

The British, at war with Napoleon, had a pressing need to increase the ranks of the Royal Navy. They boarded U.S. vessels and pressed American sailors into His Majesty's service. Adding to the turmoil, a congressional faction dubbed the "War Hawks" viewed war with Britain as potential relief from the Native American hostilities and also as a means of further expansion in Spanish Florida, since Spain was allied with Britain in the battles against Napoleon.

Telling Congress that " . . . our commerce has been plundered in every sea . . . " Madison made it clear he felt Britain was intent on destroying American commerce, while at the same time he sidelined any action against French hostilities. On June 19, Madison signed a declaration of war, passed by both houses of Congress. What wasn't known, however, was that Britain had actually revoked the practice of intercepting American ships a few days prior, and apparently the French had repealed their own restrictions on American trade.

MR. MADISON'S WAR

Unfortunately, Madison's call for preparedness had not been heeded, and the country was ill prepared for war. This brought only ridicule to the administration already facing regional differences. Northerners showed no interest in annexing Florida, a Southern conquest, and Southerners saw any move into Canada as strength added to the Northern states. New England Federalists called the War of 1812 "Mr. Madison's War."

The National Anthem

The American flag flying over Fort McHenry at daybreak inspired Francis Scott Key to write "The Star-Spangled Banner" in 1814. Key had boarded a British frigate under a flag of truce to arrange a prisoner's release, and scrawled the poem on a handbill. Later set to the tune of a popular English drinking song, it officially became the national anthem on March 3, 1931.

Although the U.S. Navy won several victories in the war's first year, 1813 saw the British navy seize many ports and capture several American ships. One American vessel—the USS *Constitution*—had earned a reputation for getting the best of British ships. In August 1812, it attacked the British ship *Guerrière*, shredding the ship's sails and rendering her dead at sea. The *Constitution* then sailed to Brazilian waters, turning the HMS *Java* into a flaming ruin. With all the heavy fire she weathered, the *Constitution* was dubbed "Old Ironsides."

BATTLES

Battles were fought along the Great Lakes and into the Canadian frontier. The Battle of Lake Erie, under Oliver Perry's command, was the turning point in the northwest for the Americans and tipped the balance of power. American and British negotiators met in Belgium to agree on settlement terms. But while peace was being procured, the British decided to invade the Gulf Coast.

Dolley Madison to the Rescue

When Dolley Madison was warned that the British were en route and was told to flee the White House, she calmly made sure that the president's papers, the national seal, and the Gilbert Stuart portrait of George Washington were sent off for safekeeping. Her actions earned her a reputation as the plucky first lady who kept her head in a crisis.

Andrew Jackson won a decisive victory over the British in the Battle of New Orleans on January 8, 1815. This was perhaps the greatest (and most unnecessary) battle of the War of 1812. News of peace and the Treaty of Ghent finally reached Jackson in March, months after the final resolution had been agreed upon on December 24,

1814. The treaty essentially restored matters to prewar conditions. Neither side left the war with more territory than it had commenced fighting with, though the United States claimed victory.

However, the war opened the west for expansion, forcing slavery to the fore as a national issue.

During the war, the British took the city of Washington, D.C., burning many government buildings, including the president's home, referred to as the White House. The British saw this torching as justifiable retaliation for the American burning of York (now Toronto), the capital of Upper Canada, the previous year.

JACKSONIAN DEMOCRACY

The Limits of Freedom

Andrew Jackson was inaugurated as the seventh president of the United States in March 1829. As a result of changes that occurred during his presidency and because of the populist rhetoric he and his supporters sometimes employed, we refer to "Jacksonian Democracy" as a broad democratic movement that became enshrined in the American political system.

In fact, Jackson's presidency was profoundly *un*democratic in some respects. Native Americans, for example, found that the federal government had no intention of honoring treaties it had signed with them. As more and more Americans looked westward for profit, the Jackson administration became committed to the removal of Native Americans from the lands promised them by previous administrations. In 1830 Congress passed the Indian Removal Act.

Court-Ordered "Justice"

In *Cherokee Nation v. Georgia* in 1831, Chief Justice Marshall created the legal justification for Indian Removal when he ruled that the Cherokee tribe did not constitute a legal nation with the standing to sue the government. They were, he wrote, a "domestic dependent nation," a definition that the government used thereafter to destroy existing treaties with the Cherokee and other tribes.

THE BATTLE WITH THE BANK

The most memorable of Jackson's conflicts while in office was with the Second Bank of the United States. At issue was the functioning of the bank as a mixed public and private institution, one that lent money regularly to the government. Jackson resented the bank as a challenge to his power and to what he saw as the sovereign right of the people to control their own financial affairs.

When in 1832 Congress passed a measure to extend the bank's charter, Jackson decided to veto it. In his veto message, he set forth what came to be the creed of Jacksonian democracy:

> In the full enjoyment of the gifts of Heaven and the fruits of superior industry, economy, and virtue, every man is equally entitled to protection by law; but when the laws undertake to add to these natural and just advantages and artificial distinctions ... to make the rich richer and the potent more powerful, the humble members of society—the farmers, mechanics, and laborers—who have neither the time nor the means of securing like favors to themselves, have a right to complain of the injustice of their Government.

The attack on the bank had support not only from poorer people but from farmers, who were in debt to it, and New York bankers, who wanted their own financial institutions to be dominant. In any event, Jackson was triumphant and was re-elected in 1832.

SLAVERY

America's Original Sin

By the mid-1800s there were many differences dividing the Northern and Southern states. The major difference lingered from the signing of the Constitution, when some statesmen opposed slavery while others clearly favored it. Slavery wasn't the only issue that divided the country, however. In the North, agricultural, commercial, and industrial development led to fast-growing cities. The North's industrial society needed labor for its economic prosperity, but the commencing wave of immigration provided a labor pool without resorting to slavery. In the South, however, the economy was dependent on foreign sales of cotton. In addition, the South opposed tariffs on imported goods, but the North's manufacturing economy demanded tariffs to stave off foreign competition.

The Dred Scott Case

In 1857, the U.S. Supreme Court decided the case of Dred Scott, a fugitive slave, who argued for his freedom after his master died when the two traveled to another state. When the Missouri state court ruled against Scott, he took his case to the Supreme Court, where Chief Justice Roger B. Taney had the final word, denying him the right to sue for his freedom, reasoning that a slave wasn't a citizen.

When slaveholding Missouri applied for statehood in 1818, there was a balance of slave states and free states, with eleven of each. Each faction viewed any attempt by the other faction to tip the scales as dangerous. Such fears delayed the annexation of Texas. Thus, Congress found a middle ground with what became known as the Missouri Compromise, enacted in 1820 and regulating the extension of slavery in the country for three decades until its repeal by the Kansas-Nebraska Act of 1854.

The Kansas-Nebraska Act authorized the creation of Kansas and Nebraska, territories west and north of Missouri, and stipulated that the inhabitants of these territories would decide the legality of slavery. The bill's sponsor, Democratic senator Stephen A. Douglas of Illinois, wanted to assure Southern support for white settlement into otherwise Native American territory. Removing the restriction on slavery's expansion ensured passage, and President Franklin Pierce signed the bill into law May 30, 1854.

With passage, however, political parties went into turmoil, and tensions between the North and South grew more passionate. The vicious fighting that resulted became known as "Bleeding Kansas," and one of the names made famous over this dispute was John Brown, a self-ordained preacher with fervor against slavery. In May 1856, Brown and his sons murdered five slave-supporting settlers at Pottawatomie Creek.

The issue and the political fallout split the Democratic Party and destroyed the badly divided Whig Party, particularly in the South. The northern Whigs joined the antislavery sentiment, forming the Republican Party in 1854.

FARMING THE LAND

The slave trade provided much-needed laborers to fill the workforce of the typical Southern plantation. Indentured servants from Europe also provided both skilled and unskilled labor to many colonies. Invention also led the way. By the mid-nineteenth century, proper drainage brought more land into cultivation, and farming implements had also advanced.

The Cotton Gin

Invented by twenty-seven-year-old Eli Whitney in 1793, the cotton gin made cleaning cottonseeds fifty times faster than by hand. Thus, cotton became king, and slavery the king's servant.

As far back as 1797, Charles Newbold, a New Jersey blacksmith, introduced the cast-iron moldboard plow. John Deere, another blacksmith, improved this plow in the 1830s, manufacturing it in steel. In 1831, twenty-two-year-old Cyrus McCormick invented the reaper, a machine that in only a few hours could cut an amount of grain that had taken two or three men a day to scythe by hand. Numerous other horse-drawn threshers, grain and grass cutters, cultivators, and other equipment made farming easier.

Advances in transportation with the construction of roads, canals, and railways meant that farmers could receive needed supplies and market their products to areas at a distance. Food stayed fresher for longer periods with the development of refrigeration in the late 1800s.

THE CRY FOR STATES' RIGHTS

Since the birth of the republic, states were fearful of tyranny and slow to release any powers to the federal government. In fact, the principle of nullification (the legal theory that a state can nullify any federal law it deems unconstitutional) was supported by many of the early founders, among them James Madison and Thomas Jefferson. The New England states nullified an unpopular embargo from 1809 to 1810, and years later, Georgia nullified federal laws relating to Native Americans.

The Dangers of Nullification

In 1830, Senator Daniel Webster warned that nullification would cause the Union to fall apart in a civil war. But in 1832, South Carolina declared a tariff null and void, forcing President Andrew Jackson to consider sending troops to enforce the tariff in the port of Charleston.

As the crisis intensified, Southern states claimed the right to nullify antislavery legislation and more and more sought to limit the power of the federal government to interfere with it.

THE UNDERGROUND RAILROAD

The antislavery faction, comprised mostly of Northerners, helped fugitive slaves reach safety in a loose, secret network dubbed "the Underground Railroad," sometimes called "the Liberty Line." This enabled runaway slaves to achieve safety in the free states or in Canada. Of course, even in free states runaway slaves would not be safe, as the federal Fugitive Slave Act under the Compromise of 1850 required that they be returned to their owners. Begun in the 1780s by Quakers, the Underground Railroad grew legendary after the 1830s. It's thought that approximately 60,000 slaves gained freedom through this lifeline.

Many hiding out in the Underground Railroad traveled at night, using the North Star for guidance. Isolated farms or towns sympathetic to a slave's plight would effectively conceal fleeing slaves. Harriet Tubman, an escaped slave, became known as the Moses of the blacks for her work in rescuing slaves and leading them to freedom.

Even under these circumstances, escaping slavery was an arduous task. Vigilant officers in search of rewards often spotted runaway slaves, seizing them as they made their passage north. But even if the slaves didn't always reach safety, their efforts did give validity to the antislavery cause, forcing many to publicly acknowledge the wrongs of slavery. Even the federal Fugitive Slave Acts of 1793 and 1850 became difficult to enforce as Northern judges restricted the rights of many a slave's master. This further enraged the Southern states, galvanizing sentiment toward Civil War.

"The Drinking Gourd"

The American folk song "Follow the Drinking Gourd" is said to have been used by slaves on the Underground Railroad as a guide. The drinking gourd referred to the constellation of the Big Dipper, found in the Northern skies.

Follow the drinking gourd.
Follow the drinking gourd.
For the old man is a-waiting
To carry you to freedom.
Follow the drinking gourd!

RAILROADS AND TELEGRAPHS

The Revolution in Communication

In the years leading up to the Civil War, the country was knit together with threads of steel. The continent-wide web of railroads and the development of the telegraph meant that the great distances that had inhibited communication and travel were suddenly gone. People and messages sped across the country at unprecedented velocities.

THE TELEGRAPH

Numerous inventions arose during the 1830s and 1840s, but none was more important to the future of the United States than the telegraph.

American Inventions in the Nineteenth Century

- Electric dynamo (1831)
- McCormick reaper (1834)
- Deere steel plow (1839)
- Sewing machine (1846)

This was the creation of Samuel Morse, originally a (not very successful) painter who turned his hand to electricity after traveling to Europe in 1832. He conceived the idea of communication that could take place by creating and disrupting a closed circuit. This would cause a small key to click in a series of patterns determined by the person sending the message and interpreted on the receiving end. Morse devised the code, bearing his name, that would make this possible, and at last demonstrated his device in 1844 by sending the message from the Supreme Court to Baltimore: "What hath God wrought?"

It was a prescient question. The telegraph revolutionized communication in a way that is hard to appreciate today (the closest we come is the development of e-mail). Before this, messages traveled no faster than a horse could gallop. Even the carrying of news across a relatively small area was a considerable accomplishment.

The telegraph, however, with instant communication, made it possible for the United States to function as a single political and social entity. Not surprisingly, its initial two chief uses were political—to convey the results of elections—and commercial. When the U.S.–Mexican War broke out in 1846, it became the first war in history in which the results of battles were transmitted via telegraph by news correspondents. By 1850, the United States could boast of more than 10,000 miles of telegraph wire.

THE COMING OF THE RAILROAD

The basic mechanism for the steam locomotive was invented in Britain in the early nineteenth century, part of the Industrial Revolution that swept across Europe. By 1828 the first miles of track were being laid, although they were modest in size and scope (the Baltimore & Ohio Railroad laid only twenty-three miles that year). By the time of Jackson's presidency, passenger train travel was becoming commonplace. By the 1830s, the United States had 3,200 miles of track—more than all European countries put together.

Suspension Bridges

John Augustus Roebling, a German immigrant and civil engineer, left his mark in Pittsburgh and New York with his wire rope used to build suspension bridges. In 1857, Roebling designed and began construction of the Brooklyn Bridge joining Manhattan with Brooklyn over the East River. Thousands celebrated its opening on May 24, 1883.

The most immediate effect of railroads was, obviously, to speed up travel time. A journey from Kentucky to Washington, D.C., that in 1806 took three weeks by 1846 had shortened to four days. But there were much broader implications for the revolution in transport:

- *Growth of cities.* Since food could now be imported to urban areas on a large scale, population in the cities increased substantially.
- *Travel by workers.* It was now possible for the workforce to travel to where they were needed, a considerable boon to the economy.
- *Cultural proliferation.* Trends and fashions spread across the country now with great rapidity, creating for the first time something approaching a national American culture.

The railroads were to have considerable military uses as well, as would become evident during the Civil War. At the war's conclusion, transportation technology continued to develop at a rapid pace. Inventions such as the automatic coupler and the airbrake (invented by George Westinghouse) improved safety each decade. In the 1880s, Westinghouse pursued his interest in rail safety, and at the age of thirty-four founded Union Switch & Signal Company in Pittsburgh. Within two years, his company was selling complete systems for switching trains from track to track and indicating the position of every train.

One of the most important strides came when George Pullman built a remarkable new railcar in 1864. These cars, given the name "Pullman cars," had sliding seats, upper berths, and comfortable heating. In addition, Fred Harvey, a Kansas restauranteur, introduced meals to the railroad. In 1894, President Grover Cleveland sent federal troops to break up a strike by railroad workers at the Pullman Palace Car Company in Chicago because the strike over pay cuts interfered with mail delivery. The strike pitted Pullman against the labor leader Eugene V. Debs and his American Railway Union, one of the first industrial unions in American history.

As the railroad phenomenon grew, presidential campaigns adopted whistle-stop tours, in which the candidate would speak from the train's rear platform. During World War II, President Franklin D. Roosevelt used a specially built railcar with armor-plated sides and three-inch-thick bulletproof windows.

MANIFEST DESTINY

From Sea to Shining Sea

The idea of Manifest Destiny—that the United States had the God-given right to expand across the North American continent—was a popular and fervently held belief in the mid-1800s. The idea justified taking Native American territory, and it incited claims to even more land.

Tensions with Mexico coincided with America's quest for expansion. Mexico, which had just won its independence from Spain, had originally encouraged U.S. settlers in Texas, but its dictator, General Antonio López de Santa Anna, later banned further U.S. immigration. And when Texas declared its own independence from Mexico in 1836, Santa Anna marched to San Antonio with a force of 3,000 men to put down the insurrection. He surrounded 200 Texans, including Davy Crockett and Jim Bowie, at the Alamo, an old abandoned mission. Refusing to surrender, the Texans held firm for ten days, but the Mexicans captured the Alamo and killed its defenders.

TEXAS GAINS INDEPENDENCE

"Remember the Alamo" became a rallying cry for the Texans who were steadfast in their quest for independence. Weeks later, while Santa Anna's troops took their afternoon siesta, Texans attacked. They were under the command of Sam Houston, who had fought against the Native Americans with Andrew Jackson in the War of 1812. By the end of the Battle of San Jacinto, the Texans captured

Santa Anna, who promised, in exchange for his life, that he'd retreat from Texas. Thus, the Republic of Texas (nicknamed the "Lone Star Republic" because its flag bore a single star) received its independence.

The Alamo As Symbol

The battle of the Alamo had little military importance, but has become a symbol of fighting against overwhelming odds. The story has been told in songs, movies, novels, and (mostly bad) poetry. Today the remains of the Alamo are a popular tourist destination in San Antonio, Texas.

Sam Houston immediately asked for Texas to be annexed to the United States, but as the balance of states stood at the time, there were thirteen states opposed to slavery and thirteen states in favor of it. Northerners felt that admitting Texas, where slavery was legal, would tip the balance of power in favor of the South. Thus, annexation was tabled until President John Tyler succeeded in pushing a joint resolution through Congress allowing Texas to join the Union in 1845.

THE MEXICAN-AMERICAN WAR

When annexation occurred, Mexico severed all diplomatic ties to the United States. Mexicans were even more outraged when U.S. officials insisted that the Rio Grande be used as the southern border of Texas. Thus, border skirmishes ensued even as the new president, James Polk, offered to purchase California and New Mexico and to assume

Mexico's debts in exchange for the Rio Grande border. When rumors of a Mexican invasion caught the capital's attention, the president sent General Zachary Taylor and 3,500 troops to the Rio Grande to defend Texas. After Mexicans killed several of Taylor's men, Polk asked Congress to declare war, which it promptly did.

The U.S. soldiers who marched across the dry ground became covered with a white dust, similar in color and texture to Mexican adobes. Soon, Mexicans dubbed their opponents "dobies" or doughboys, and the name stuck for generations of soldiers.

It didn't take long to capture California, and Americans also forced a Mexican surrender at Monterrey. Yet the war effort met with criticism, for some saw this as an aggressive, unprovoked war on disputed territory. Undeterred, President Polk ordered troops south to capture Mexico City. Shortly thereafter, both sides reached peace.

Thoreau in Jail

Protesters against the Mexican War claimed it was immoral, proslavery, and against Republican values. Henry David Thoreau refused to pay his state (Massachusetts) taxes in protest and was placed in jail. Inspired by his arrest, Thoreau wrote *Civil Disobedience*, which was studied by many, including Mahatma Gandhi and Martin Luther King Jr.

After two years of fighting, the Treaty of Guadalupe Hidalgo resulted in Mexico's ceding California and large stretches of the Southwest to the United States, as well as its acceptance of the Rio Grande border. In return, the United States paid the Mexican government $15 million and assumed unpaid claims by U.S. citizens against Mexico. Zachary Taylor emerged as a hero and was elected president in 1848.

GO WEST, YOUNG MAN

After the Louisiana Purchase spurred westward expansion in the early 1800s, the country experienced the continued growth of its boundaries. Lieutenant Zebulon Pike, an army officer, led a group from Saint Louis into Minnesota. Pike won command of a Southwest expedition that took him far into Spanish-held lands between 1806 and 1807. In what is now known as Colorado, the lieutenant discovered a mountain 14,110 feet (4,301 meters) high, now bearing the name Pikes Peak.

In 1818 and 1842, treaties settled Canadian border disputes with Britain from northern Maine to the Continental Divide. England and America's disputed control of the Oregon Country was settled in 1846, with the United States gaining sovereignty of the region south of the 49th parallel.

Around this time, members of a religious sect founded by Joseph Smith in 1830 sought isolation in the West, as they had been hounded in Ohio, Missouri, then Illinois and Iowa. Mormons, or members of the Church of Jesus Christ of Latter-day Saints, practiced polygamy and roused growing suspicion. In 1847, a group of Mormons ventured over the prairie through the Rocky Mountains until they reached the dreary flats beside the Great Salt Lake in Utah. Over the next several years, thousands followed the Mormon trail their leader had blazed. They called this homeland Zion, and like the Israelites of old, they made their desert bloom. By 1860, approximately 12,000 Mormons lived in the Salt Lake City environs.

THE GOLD RUSH

A Shining Fantasy

On January 24, 1848, just days before Mexico signed the treaty giving California to the United States, men working at a sawmill in the Sacramento Valley struck gold along the American River. Mill owner John Sutter implored his workers to keep the discovery quiet, but news spread, particularly from those who stood to profit. Samuel Brannan was one such shrewd merchant, who stocked his store near Sutter's mill with mining supplies before alerting others to the potential for riches.

By spring, chaos erupted as men quit their jobs, leaving ghost towns in their wake. Hundreds of soldiers abandoned their posts, and in San Francisco harbor, sailors literally left their ships to rot as everyone flocked to the frenzy of finding gold.

The Gold Standard Today

U.S. money is no longer backed by gold. The gold standard lasted until 1971 when President Nixon announced that the United States would no longer exchange dollars for gold. Now the United States is on a system of fiat money, which is used only as a medium of exchange.

GOLD FEVER

Although it began in the spring of 1848, the gold rush grew slowly at first. It wasn't until 1849 that the largest numbers (tens of thousands) of people flooded across the continent and from all around the globe to converge on the area that would become California. Thus, those in hot pursuit of the precious metal became known as "forty-niners."

Of those who trekked west, few struck it rich, but many stayed on to establish themselves in farming or business, increasing California's population nearly tenfold between 1848 and 1853. In 1850, California was admitted as a state.

Other Gold Rushes

Gold rushes also took place in Colorado, Nevada, Montana, Arizona, New Mexico, Idaho, Oregon, and Alaska.

Wherever a gold strike was made, miners gathered to build a camp or community that usually had a saloon and a gambling house, and very few women or children. Miners lived in shanties they could easily abandon when the gold ran out and everyone pulled up stakes to head for the next strike. Frontier justice reigned, and each camp set forth its own rules on the size of the gold claim that an individual could possess, and the way it should be registered. Sheriffs administered the codes, and justice was harsh and swift.

By 1851 industrial mining became the trend and organized businesses with more advanced technology replaced individual efforts, and by the late 1850s, the California gold rush was over. Four decades later, others, in spite of the biting wind and frigid cold, trekked to Alaska when rich strikes were made near Nome and Fairbanks.

LINCOLN'S ELECTION

Lurching Toward War

Abraham Lincoln was born on February 12, 1809, in a log cabin that his father built in Kentucky. His youth was filled with hunting, fishing, and chores. Because land titles were disputed in Kentucky, Abe's father moved the family to Pigeon Creek, Indiana (near Gentryville today), where the federal government was selling land. Two years after the family settled in this thriving frontier community, Abe's mother died in an epidemic. The next year, Abe's father married a widow with three children, and Abe seemed to bond well with his stepmother.

Abe learned at a young age to wield an ax to clear the frontier forest, and he attended a log cabin school when he wasn't tending to chores. Though the lad had less than one year of formal education, his stepmother encouraged his thirst for knowledge. Lincoln learned to read, write, and do simple arithmetic at an early age, and it's said that a book about George Washington made a deep impression on him. With his family's move to Illinois, Abe helped his father build a log cabin. That year, he attended a political rally and spoke on behalf of one of the candidates.

Logrolling

The practice of supporting the projects of other legislators in return for their support became known as *logrolling*, a term derived from a game of skill, especially among lumberjacks, in which two competitors try to balance on a floating log while spinning it with their feet.

At a lanky six-foot-four, Lincoln's appearance was awkward, especially given his long arms and big hands. He held various jobs, but because he could read and write, he was called on to draw up legal papers for the less literate around him. When Lincoln expressed his views, he did so with a grace and discernment that caught people's attention.

LINCOLN ENTERS POLITICS

In the spring of 1832, Lincoln decided to run for a seat in the Illinois House of Representatives. Before the election, he volunteered in the suppression of a rebellion by Native Americans led by Chief Black Hawk, though he saw no actual fighting. Despite a platform of better schools, roads, and canals, Lincoln was defeated, and he began a venture with a general store, followed by his job as a postmaster, a position that gave him ample time to read ravenously, especially newspapers.

Now better known, Lincoln ran for the Illinois legislature in 1834. He was elected then and subsequently every two years, and he studied law between legislative sessions. This experience as a state legislator sharpened his political savvy. Lincoln's first public stand on slavery, which he'd encountered years earlier when he viewed a slave auction, came in 1837 when the Illinois legislature voted to condemn abolition societies that wanted to end the practice by any means. Although Lincoln was opposed to slavery, he also felt strongly that extreme measures were not necessary and that lawful conduct could end the practice.

Though Lincoln became a licensed lawyer in 1836, and continued as a state legislator, economic achievement and personal contentment didn't follow. Some said he was plunged into sadness by the death of Ann Rutledge, the woman he loved, and that a period of melancholy marked his adult years. Others believe this romance was a myth. He proposed marriage to another woman who turned him down. It wasn't until he met Mary Todd in 1840 that courtship blossomed, and the two were married two years later. Though she was perhaps unstable, Lincoln remained devoted to her, and she in turn supported his political rise.

CONGRESSMAN LINCOLN

The ambitious legislator and lawyer soon looked beyond Illinois to the U.S. Congress, and he was elected in 1846 to the House of Representatives. Despite the difficulties of being a freshman congressman, Lincoln never lost confidence in his abilities. He opposed the Mexican-American War begun by President Polk. In 1847, he called on Polk for proof of the president's insistence that the war began when Mexicans shed American blood on American soil. According to Lincoln, "That soil was not ours; and Congress did not annex or attempt to annex it." Lincoln voted for a resolution that declared the war unnecessary. Once war was declared, however, Lincoln supported all appropriations, despite his private opinions.

Lincoln resumed his law practice after serving one term in Congress. Travel between county seats allowed him to reflect, read, and mingle with other lawyers. Though he sometimes lacked time to prepare for cases, he made up for it with oratory skills far greater than many of his peers.

LINCOLN'S ANTISLAVERY SENTIMENTS GROW

Lincoln was outraged by passage of the Kansas-Nebraska Act in 1854, a measure that allowed the territories to decide the issue of slavery for themselves. Democratic senator Stephen Douglas was the author of the act, and Abe Lincoln's passion for the plight of slaves rose to the surface. When Douglas defended the Kansas-Nebraska Act in October of that year, Lincoln spoke the next day, attacking the act with well-researched arguments that forced citizens to contemplate not only the political ramifications of slavery but also the moral ones.

Words of Wisdom

"If the Negro is a man, why then my ancient faith teaches me that 'all men are created equal,' and that there can be no moral right in connection with one man's making a slave of another."

—Abraham Lincoln

As impassioned as his conviction was that slavery was wrong and a national problem to contend with, Lincoln remained fairly non-judgmental regarding the South. " . . . I will not undertake to judge our brethren of the South," Lincoln said in what became known as his Peoria, Illinois, speech.

By 1856, the Whig Party that Lincoln belonged to had died out, and the young politician officially identified himself as a Republican. Soon, the slavery issue was gaining national momentum with the *Dred Scott* case and memories of Bleeding Kansas. As Senator

Stephen Douglas ran for re-election, the Republicans nominated Abraham Lincoln to oppose him. Accepting the nomination, Lincoln used his harshest words, declaring, "A house divided against itself cannot stand. I believe this government cannot endure permanently half slave and half free. I do not expect the Union to be dissolved; I do not expect the house to fall; but I do expect it will cease to be divided. It will become all one thing, or all the other."

John Brown's Rebellion

Abolitionist John Brown grew so obsessed with winning freedom for slaves that on October 16, 1859, he and approximately twenty others incited an uprising. Federal troops commanded by Robert E. Lee retaliated, killing about half the group, wounding Brown and taking him prisoner. Brown was brought to trial and convicted of treason, murder, and criminal conspiracy. He was hanged on December 2, 1859.

THE LINCOLN-DOUGLAS DEBATES

In a series of face-to-face debates that captivated Illinois citizens, the two Senate candidates debated the morality of slavery. By now Lincoln was well known as an extraordinary political stump speaker.

Though Lincoln was confident he could defeat Douglas, the Democratic majority won, re-electing Douglas. Lincoln handled his loss with grace, glad he could speak out on a truly crucial issue. He wrote to a friend, " ... I believe I have made some remarks which will tell for the cause of civil liberty long after I am gone."

The debates launched Lincoln onto the national stage, giving him opportunities to speak in other states. His moderate views won him praise as he insisted the Republican Party was not one solely of Northern origin but that it encompassed the South as well. After speaking in New York, Lincoln became the leading contender for the Republican presidential nomination in 1860.

When the party convened, they did in fact select Lincoln as their presidential nominee. With the Democratic Party split, Lincoln felt confident of victory. Though he won only 40 percent of the popular vote, he received the majority of electoral votes (though none in the South) and won the race to become the sixteenth president of the United States.

The Homestead Act

The Homestead Act of 1862 gave settlers 160 acres of federal land for a nominal filing fee if they would farm it for five years. This federally owned land included property in all states except the original thirteen and Maine, Vermont, West Virginia, Kentucky, Tennessee, and Texas.

Southern militants had already threatened to secede from the Union if Lincoln was elected president. Sure enough, when election results became known, South Carolina became the first Southern state to leave the Union in December 1860. By February, several other states followed as they developed their own government.

LINCOLN TAKES OFFICE

As he bid farewell to Illinois, Lincoln remained hopeful that peace could be restored. "Today I leave you," he told friends. "I go to assume a task more difficult than that which devolved upon George

Washington." And with additional words reflecting his belief in God, he asked his followers to pray for the country and his efforts.

Because rumors of a possible assassination plot were rampant, he quietly sneaked into Washington at night for his inauguration on March 4, 1861. Ironically, Lincoln was sworn in as president by Chief Justice Roger B. Taney, who also issued the *Dred Scott* decision—a deed that spurred the crisis that would consume Lincoln's presidency.

FORT SUMTER

The Fateful Lightning

As tensions rose between the North and South, citizens could no longer deny the imminent outbreak of war as their new president, Abraham Lincoln, took office. As the Southern states seceded, the Confederates seized most of the federal forts within their borders. Only four remained under Union control: Fort Sumter (Charleston, South Carolina), Fort Jefferson, Fort Pickens, and Fort Taylor (all in Florida).

CREATION OF THE CONFEDERACY

Following South Carolina's secession, Mississippi, Florida, Alabama, Georgia, Louisiana, and Texas adopted similar ordinances. The seceding states sent representatives to a convention in Montgomery, Alabama, where they adopted a provisional constitution, gave themselves a name, and chose a president of their own: Jefferson Davis of Mississippi. Thus, the Confederate States of America (known as the Confederacy) was born.

STATES THAT SECEDED FROM THE UNION		
STATE	SECESSION DATE	READMISSION DATE
South Carolina	December 20, 1860	June 25, 1868
Mississippi	January 9, 1861	February 23, 1870
Florida	January 10, 1861	June 25, 1868
Alabama	January 11, 1861	June 25, 1868
Georgia	January 19, 1861	June 25, 1868*
Louisiana	January 26, 1861	June 25, 1868

*Georgia was readmitted a second time on July 15, 1870.

STATES THAT SECEDED FROM THE UNION		
STATE	SECESSION DATE	READMISSION DATE
Texas	February 1, 1861	March 30, 1870
Virginia	April 17, 1861	January 26, 1870
Arkansas	May 6, 1861	June 22, 1868
North Carolina	May 20, 1861	June 25, 1868
Tennessee	June 8, 1861	July 24, 1866

PREPARING FOR WAR

After selecting cabinet members who came from other Southern states (and thus, he hoped, making it representative of the Confederacy as a whole), Jefferson Davis turned his attention to the necessary preparations for the impending conflict with the North (Union). Confederates had already seized eleven federal forts and arsenals in the South, and they had caused trouble at Fort Sumter in Charleston, South Carolina. Shortly after he took office, President Lincoln sent reinforcements to Fort Sumter.

Economic Weakness

When created, the Confederacy had a population of almost 9 million, including nearly 4 million slaves. But that paled by comparison to the Union population of approximately 22 million. Land values were higher in the North, as was economic strength, making the South extremely dependent on Europe for many material items. A basic lack of resources forced the Confederacy to levy taxes and deal with rising inflation. Southern railroads proved to be inadequate, and the South also lacked manufacturing equipment to make large field guns and even basic military equipment.

The Confederate government was in a state of constant turmoil, with judges from the various state courts interfering in military matters. However, Davis did appoint General Robert E. Lee as commander of the Army of Northern Virginia, and he remained true to his task until the bitter end.

FIRE ON FORT SUMTER

As moderate as Lincoln tried to be in his policies, there was no fence-sitting when Confederate rebels fired on Fort Sumter in South Carolina in April 1861. He had to act swiftly. Fort Sumter, which lay at the entrance to the Charleston harbor, remained under the command of Major Robert Anderson and a small detachment of federal troops. It was by far the most important of the four forts remaining under Union control.

Harriet Beecher Stowe

Harriet Beecher Stowe, an American writer and abolitionist, wrote a powerful novel—Uncle Tom's Cabin—that precipitated the Civil War as it strengthened the antislavery movement. Legend has it that when President Lincoln met Harriet Beecher Stowe, he said, "So you're the little woman who wrote the book that started this great war."

Reluctantly, because he feared igniting war, President Lincoln sent supplies to reinforce Fort Sumter, but the Confederates blocked the harbor. With orders from President Jefferson Davis of the Confederacy, General Beauregard demanded that the Union surrender the fort. When Major Anderson ignored the ultimatum, Confederate fire erupted on April 12, 1861, and Anderson had little choice but to surrender.

The Civil War had begun.

FOUR YEARS AT WAR

Neither side knew at the initial firing that the Civil War would last four years and rank among the bloodiest wars ever fought. Although the issue of slavery loomed large, it didn't by any means diminish the goal of reconciling the country. Lincoln refused to recognize the legitimacy of the Confederate government, insisting instead that it was a rebellion that could be quelled.

The Growth of War Technology

One reason the war produced so many casualties was because military technology had outpaced the development of tactics. Thus, improvements in the design and manufacturing of rifles produced guns that could shoot farther and straighter than previously, but troops continued to rely on massed firepower, often standing upright in plain sight when shooting at the enemy. Not surprisingly, they were mown down in great numbers.

Lincoln's resolve was to the North's advantage, for he became the towering symbol in body and in deed of the nation's strength. While the North enjoyed other advantages in terms of population, troops, and resources, the South found it far easier to defend its territory than to invade. The North had to push forth, carrying battles south in order to cripple the South's capacity to wage war. Of course, this proved to be more costly and time-consuming. Strategically, the South felt it could learn from the example set in the Revolutionary War: to win meant exhausting the other side, dragging out the conflict until the North would no longer want to commit resources to the effort.

Bitterness Still Remains

Among many in the South, the issues over which the Civil War (or, as it's called in the South, the War of Northern Aggression) was fought continue to resonate. In many areas, Confederate flags fly as a symbol of Southern heritage, despite bitter protests from African Americans, who consider the flag a symbol of slavery.

Early in the Civil War, Lincoln removed Brigadier General Irvin McDowell from his command of the federal army and placed Major General George B. McClellan in the role. While McClellan restored morale and raised the caliber of the fighting forces, he lacked decisiveness.

FAMOUS BATTLES IN THE SOUTH

Although at the outbreak of the war the Union may have had expectations of quick and easy victory, the first Union offensive put an end to them.

In July 1861, at the First Battle of Bull Run, or what the South called First Manassas, the Confederates used some of the brightest and best in military talent to defeat the Union soldiers marching into Virginia. Not only were McDowell's troops inexperienced, not to mention threatened with Confederate forces so near Washington, D.C., but they also suffered from overconfidence.

The Confederate army of General Beauregard maintained a line along Bull Run Creek (or Manassas Junction), and the Virginia brigade led by Thomas J. Jackson was at the line's center. His stubborn defense earned him the nickname "Stonewall Jackson," for his troops remained standing like a stone wall.

In February 1862, Union gunboats led by Commodore Andrew Foote steamed up the Tennessee River to reach Fort Henry, where the plan called for an amphibious attack. Ulysses S. Grant led forces on land, but the muddy roads they traversed slowed them. Foote grew impatient and fired, wreaking havoc with the fort's walls. With floodwaters flowing in, the Southern forces raised the white flag.

Most of the escaping Confederates sought shelter at Fort Donelson on the Columbia River. Grant's army pursued them by land and despite lacking reinforcements, they broke Confederate lines and caused acting General Buckner to surrender. Buckner, who had known Grant before the Civil War, expected generous surrender terms. That was wishful thinking, for Grant demanded unconditional and immediate surrender, earning him the nickname "Unconditional Surrender" Grant.

Prisoners of War

More than 150 prisons for captured soldiers were established during the Civil War. All were filled beyond capacity, with inmates crowded into camps and shelters with meager provisions. Although precise figures may never be known, an estimated 56,000 men perished in Civil War prisons, a casualty rate far greater than any battle during the war.

In early April 1862, Grant was in a holding pattern in Tennessee while he waited for another Union commander to join him in a campaign toward Corinth, Mississippi. However, Confederate commander Albert Johnston's troops struck Grant's army by surprise.

Grant lost approximately 13,000 men and the Confederates almost as many in a bloody battle known as Shiloh (ironically, a Hebrew word suggesting "place of peace").

THE PENINSULAR CAMPAIGN

Also that spring, with General McClellan in charge, the Union army advanced by way of the peninsula between the James and York Rivers in Virginia in order to reach Richmond, the Confederate capital. But McClellan was not a decisive leader, and he delayed the assault on Richmond. The resulting Seven Days Battles, fought in late June 1862, led to an alarming number of casualties. Lincoln's administration held McClellan responsible for not taking Richmond, while McClellan blamed the president for not sending reinforcements.

Though most of the nation's attention was focused on the peninsula, the Union needed to gain control of New Orleans if it ever wanted to navigate the Mississippi River and effectively blockade the South. In April 1862, Flag Officer David Farragut, with a squadron of ships carrying federal troops, started up the Mississippi and arrived on April 25, demanding surrender. As the Confederates numbered only 3,000, they gave up easily, inflicting a painful loss on the South.

THREE UNION LOSSES

In 1862 and early 1863, Confederate forces inflicted three major defeats on the Union's Army of the Potomac, while the Union scored one significant victory:

1. Second Bull Run/Second Manassas (June 1862)—Confederate victory
2. Antietam/Sharpsburg (September 1862)—Union victory
3. Fredericksburg (December 1862)—Confederate victory
4. Chancellorsville (April 1863)—Confederate victory

After each battle, Lincoln replaced the commander of the army—John Pope (Second Manassas) with George McClellan (Antietam) with Ambrose Burnside (Fredericksburg) with Joseph Hooker (Chancellorsville). After the latter's defeat, Lincoln appointed George Meade commander of the Army of the Potomac.

NORTHERN FIGHTING

Robert E. Lee's motive for winning a battle in the North was to finally convince foreign governments to back the South, and he believed that sympathizers in the Border States would also join the Confederate cause. As his army headed into Maryland, they were a pathetic sight—dirty, hungry, and often barefoot. Nervous about Confederate troops in his backyard, Lincoln relieved Pope of his command, giving McClellan, or "Little Mac," another chance to fend off Lee's troops.

In planning his battle, which occurred near Sharpsburg, Maryland, McClellan had a stunning piece of good fortune: a Confederate soldier left behind a precious piece of military intelligence—General Lee's troop orders—and McClellan received them. The Union corporal who stumbled on the information turned it over to McClellan, but in another surprise, a Southern sympathizer tipped off General Lee that the North knew of his plans. As a result, Lee pulled back his forces, and instead of attacking quickly, the cautious-as-ever McClellan hesitated, believing that Lee outnumbered him. In the fighting that September 1862, McClellan drove Lee back into Virginia in the bloodiest one-day battle ever fought. The Battle of Antietam, or Sharpsburg as the South called it, cost both sides dearly, but the outcome was a Union victory.

GETTYSBURG

The Terrible Swift Sword

By summer 1863, General Lee's army was at its fighting peak, anxious to threaten Northern territory. Lee commanded his army through Gettysburg, Pennsylvania, in order to march farther north.

Early on July 1, a group of Rebels in search of badly needed shoes stumbled on Northern cavalry units. By midday, Lee sent in his own reinforcements, who drove the Union away. Soon, blue-clad soldiers were spotted traipsing through Gettysburg.

Chamberlain at Little Round Top

A key role in the defense of Little Round Top was played by the 20th Maine under the command of Joshua Chamberlain. When his regiment ran low on ammunition, Chamberlain, in a daring move, swung his left wing around and launched a bayonet charge at the surprised Confederates, driving them off the hill.

Chamberlain was present at Lee's surrender to Grant at Appomattox in Virginia and, as the Confederate soldiers prepared to surrender, he ordered his troops to "present arms" to show their respect for the defeated foe.

Lee tried to get General Richard Ewell to seize Cemetery Hill, just south of the town, but Ewell was too cautious, and the Union set up a line along the ridge during the night. Union commander General George Meade formed a fishhook line to the southeast whereby the curve of the hook was Cemetery Hill with the shaft running down Cemetery Ridge. Lee ordered charges to the right and left flanks, hoping to crush the Union line.

Confederates did capture Devil's Den, a boulder-strewn area in front of the hill known as Little Round Top. Had they put cannons atop Little Round Top, they could have blasted the Union line. Once the Rebels were spotted, however, fighting recommenced, and Little Round Top was saved.

The Rebels had charged Cemetery Ridge and Cemetery Hill, but they hadn't forced the Union troops from there. Meade chose to stay on the defensive, repeatedly repulsing Lee's assaults.

War in Kentucky

During August and September 1862, the Confederate army invaded Kentucky, a slave state that had not seceded from the Union. Kentuckians were divided, and it wasn't uncommon to have people from the same community enlist in both the Confederate and Union armies. They clashed at the Battle of Perryville on October 8, 1862. Neither side could claim victory, but the Confederates retreated.

General James Longstreet of the Confederacy had warned Lee not to attack the Union's center of the line. On the third day, in what became known as Pickett's Charge, Confederates sent 15,000 men advancing over more than a mile toward the Union line. The charge failed to break through, and the Confederates retreated with heavy casualties. In the scorching heat of those three July days, the Union fielded 83,300 men and sustained 23,000 casualties. The Confederacy fielded 75,100 men and sustained 28,100 casualties.

LINCOLN'S GETTYSBURG ADDRESS

Lincoln was called upon to deliver a few remarks on November 19, 1863, to dedicate a military cemetery at Gettysburg. He delivered his address following those of Edward Everett, a distinguished speaker in his own right. While Everett spoke for two hours, the president said just 268 words. But they were profound and masterful, imparting another persuasive vision for America:

Four score and seven years ago our fathers brought forth on this continent, a new nation, conceived in Liberty, and dedicated to the proposition that all men are created equal.

Now we are engaged in a great civil war, testing whether the nation, or any nation so conceived and so dedicated, can long endure. We are met on a great battlefield of that war. We have come to dedicate a portion of that field, as a final resting place for those who here gave their lives that that nation might live. It is altogether fitting and proper that we should do this.

But, in a larger sense, we cannot dedicate—we cannot consecrate—we cannot hallow—this ground. The brave men, living and dead, who struggled here, have consecrated it, far above our poor power to add or detract. The world will little note nor long remember what we say here, but it can never forget what they did here. It is for us the living, rather, to be dedicated here to the unfinished work which they who fought here have thus far so nobly advanced. It is rather for us to be here dedicated to the great task remaining before us—that from these honored dead we take increased devotion to that cause for which they gave the last full measure of devotion—that we here highly resolve that these dead shall not have died in vain—that this nation, under

God, shall have a new birth of freedom—and that government of the people, by the people, for the people, shall not perish from the earth.

THE POLITICAL CLIMATE

Lincoln, despite his opposition to slavery, saw his main objective as saving the Union. In the early stages of the war, Lincoln trod carefully so as not to offend slaveholding Border States, key to the North's military advantage. After McClellan's victory at the Battle of Antietam in 1862, though, Lincoln felt he had enough political force to take an initial step toward abolition. On January 1, 1863, Lincoln signed the Emancipation Proclamation, freeing the slaves in the seceding states.

Forever Free

Lincoln pushed for the Thirteenth Amendment, which made up for the limitations of the Emancipation Proclamation: it barred slavery from the United States in perpetuity. Later, it became a condition that Southern states had to accept the amendment to be readmitted to the Union. It became law in January 1865.

The proclamation didn't apply to the Border States, which were not in rebellion against the Union, though Lincoln did urge voluntary compensated emancipation. In fact, Lincoln did not have the power to free slaves except under the powers granted during war to seize enemy property.

... I do order and declare that all persons held as slaves within [the seceding states], are, and henceforeward shall be free; and that the Executive government of the United States, including the military and naval authorities thereof, will recognize and maintain the freedom of said persons.

Usually, Lincoln signed bills in abbreviated form using "A. Lincoln." However, he signed his full signature onto the Emancipation Proclamation, and said to those cabinet officers standing near, "Gentlemen, I never, in my life, felt more certain that I was doing right than in signing this paper."

Lincoln's proclamation gave slaves a beacon of hope. As they spotted Union troops approaching their towns, slaves refused to work for their masters. Further along in his address, Lincoln invited slaves to join the Union army. By the end of the Civil War, one Union soldier in eight was African-American. This hastened the South's demise, and the governments of France and Great Britain took notice as well.

GRANT AND LEE

The Great Antagonists

On the day Lee withdrew his forces from Gettysburg, Lincoln received word that General Ulysses S. Grant had captured Vicksburg, Mississippi, a key Confederate fort along the Mississippi River. Throughout the winter and spring, Grant's army had tried one tactic after another to attack the city, but with stump-clogged canals, tangled forests, massive flooding, and Confederate fighting power, Grant's men had to literally dig their way to Rebel lines, keeping up a steady bombardment and forcing civilians to go underground for safety. With no relief army in sight, the Confederates asked Grant for surrender terms, and on July 4, 1863, the Rebels stacked their arms before marching out of their fallen city. Grant's victory opened the Mississippi River to the Union and effectively broke the Confederacy in two.

By the end of 1863, the Union had achieved two main objectives—control of the Mississippi River, which split the South in two, and a strangling blockade of Southern ports. Severely lacking, however, was a coordinated strategy to finish the war, until in March 1864, Lincoln selected General Grant to command the Northern troops.

THE SOUTH SURRENDERS

General Grant gave General William Tecumseh Sherman full command of the West, while he himself moved east to lead the Army of the Potomac against General Lee's Confederate forces. His strategy:

attack the South's strong armies rather than take key Southern cities. While focused on Lee, Sherman's march through Georgia went after General Joseph Johnston's force of 45,000 men. While en route, he destroyed much of the Confederate infrastructure, especially the vital rail and industrial strength of Atlanta. On September 1, 1864, Sherman succeeded in his mission, sending a telegram to the president that "Atlanta is ours, and fairly won." The capture did much to solidify Lincoln's re-election.

Meanwhile, Lee's Army of Northern Virginia spent much of the fall and winter of 1864–65 hunkered down in trenches.

Lee's attempt to launch an offensive failed, and with Grant commandeering Lee's last rail supply line, Lee advised Jefferson Davis to move his Confederate government out of Richmond. Finally, desertion, disease, near-starvation, and the Union's relentless attacks brought the Confederacy to its knees.

Calling a truce, Lee asked for a meeting with Grant to discuss surrender terms. On the afternoon of April 9, 1865, the two generals met at Appomattox. In his offer to Lee, Grant stated that Confederate forces could keep their own horses, baggage, and side arms, returning home with the assurance that U.S. authorities would not harm them. Grant even made arrangements to feed Lee's troops before the two parted.

Lee's army stacked its arms and surrendered battle flags on April 12, 1865, though it took until June for all Confederate forces to lay down their arms. When the Union forces gloated over their victory with artillery salutes, Grant demanded they stop. Later he wrote, "We did not want to exult over their downfall. The war is over. The rebels are our countrymen again."

RECONSTRUCTION AND REACTION

Rebuilding a Nation

After the war, the Republican majority in Congress pushed through the Fourteenth Amendment, which defined American citizenship to include all former slaves and declared that individual states could not unlawfully deny citizens their rights and privileges. As with the Thirteenth Amendment, seceding states had to adopt the Fourteenth Amendment to be readmitted. The required three-fourths of the states ratified the amendment on July 9, 1868, though the measure had passed Congress two years earlier.

The Fifteenth Amendment, granting African-American men the right to vote, also took a two-year path to ratification. It was presented to the states in 1868, and Southern states grudgingly passed the measure. In the 1890s, former Confederate states required African Americans to take literacy tests as a requirement for voting. Since few slaves were literate at the time, this all but eliminated voting among this group until the modern civil rights movement protested these strictures. Interestingly, this amendment said nothing about affording women the right to vote, an issue that wasn't addressed until 1920.

The Civil War in Numbers

- 620,000 soldiers died in combat
- 180,000 African-American soldiers served in the war
- 674,000 soldiers captured
- $5 billion in destroyed property (in 1860 dollars)

In addition to the legislative fallout from the war, it created social wounds that never completely healed. It did, however, end slavery, making many believe the moral objectives of the war were indeed accomplished.

ONE FATEFUL NIGHT AT THE THEATER

On Good Friday, April 14, 1865, Lincoln and his wife were to attend a performance of *Our American Cousin* at Ford's Theatre in Washington, D.C. At approximately 10:30 P.M. and at a moment when all eyes were focused on the stage, John Wilkes Booth, a Southern sympathizer, crept into the poorly protected presidential box and fired his pistol at Lincoln's head. The president slumped into his seat, unconscious, while Booth leaped to the stage shouting, "*Sic semper tyrannis*," the Virginia state motto, which means "Thus ever to tyrants." Though he had injured his foot, Booth succeeded in escaping.

Lincoln was taken to a lodging house across the street, where Mrs. Lincoln, cabinet members, and friends waited through the night for doctors to perform a miracle that never happened. On Saturday, April 15, 1865, Lincoln was pronounced dead, and within hours Vice President Andrew Johnson was sworn in as president. This was the first presidential assassination in United States history.

Booth was captured twelve days later in a shack near Bowling Green, Virginia. When he refused to surrender to authorities, they set the barn ablaze. Some say that Booth was struck by a sniper's shot, and others assert that he pulled a gun on himself. Regardless, Booth was dragged out of the inferno and died shortly thereafter. His coconspirators went on trial for aiding the assassin. They were tried and convicted by a military tribunal rather than a civil court.

MENDING AMERICA

Thrust into the presidency after a mere forty-one days on the job as second-in-command, Andrew Johnson tried to reunite the bitterly divided land.

Johnson shared Lincoln's view favoring leniency toward the Southern states, but a group of congressmen called the Radical Republicans resented Johnson's Reconstruction policies. Reconstruction was the official name given the rebuilding process following the American Civil War. It forced the country to grapple with pressing questions that came up after Southern defeat and the abolition of slavery:

- Should there be punishment for the Confederate rebellion?
- What rights would be granted to the newly freed slaves?
- What criteria did Confederate states need to meet before being judged as "reconstructed"?
- How would the Southern economy survive and prosper without its traditional labor base?

Johnson offered amnesty to all who took the oath of allegiance (and if the Confederates had postwar wealth surpassing $20,000, they had to apply for a pardon). He returned plantations to their former owners, and he sought to restore political rights to the Southern states as soon as possible, with each state drafting a new constitution. Of course, these constitutions had to outlaw slavery and disavow secession. Bitter over their defeat, many Southerners still restricted the rights of former slaves, and this angered Northerners who felt that Johnson was selling out to the South.

Seward's Folly

Johnson's secretary of state, William H. Seward, signed a treaty with Russia for the purchase of land that would become Alaska. Critics called him mad to pay $7.2 million for unexplored territory to the north. Seward reached the deal in 1867, and it was quickly ridiculed as "Seward's Folly." It wasn't until the Alaskan gold rush years later that Seward's shrewd purchase would be appreciated.

DISSENSION GROWS

The faction against President Johnson grew in its belief that the Union victory had to stand for more than simple restoration. The Republican majority in the House of Representatives refused to seat their colleagues sent by Southern states. Lengthy debate ensued, with Congress passing its version of the First Reconstruction Act in March 1867 over Johnson's veto. Southern states were given a military commander to oversee the writing of new state constitutions that would allow all adult males to vote, regardless of race. If states ratified their new constitutions along with the Fourteenth Amendment, they would be readmitted to the Union.

Compromise eventually won out, but the damage had been done. In 1868, Andrew Johnson became the first president to be impeached and put on trial by the Senate, even though no constitutional grounds existed for his impeachment. Johnson was spared from removal by a margin of one vote. But his presidency was effectively over, based on the political disagreements stemming from his Reconstruction policies.

CHANGES IN THE SOUTH

While the U.S. War Department created the Freedmen's Bureau in 1865 to help former slaves find jobs and obtain an education, many Southern whites did what they could to keep African Americans poor and powerless. Confederate war veterans formed the Ku Klux Klan, originally a social organization, which quickly became a violent vigilante group preventing freedmen from voting. This hate group originated in Pulaski, Tennessee, and its members, often dressed in white robes with pointed hoods, spread terror as they rode on horseback at night.

Radical Republicans in Congress such as Benjamin Butler urged President Ulysses S. Grant to take action against the Ku Klux Klan. Congress passed the Ku Klux Act and it became law in 1871. This gave the president the power to intervene in troubled states. Shortly thereafter, the organization practically disappeared. The founding of the second Ku Klux Klan in 1915 was inspired by, among other things, an anti-immigrant and anti-Semitic agenda and a glorified version of the original Klan presented in the film *The Birth of a Nation*.

Though treated as second-class citizens, African Americans eagerly sought to make a better life for themselves, forming their own churches and other institutions. Most continued to vote Republican, but by the mid-1870s Democrats returned to power in some Southern states. This political transition confirmed Republican fears that Democratic victories would sometimes lead to a reversal of Reconstruction accomplishments. Black school funding was slashed, and over many decades to come, a rigid segregation policy pervaded the South. As a result, Southern blacks began their migration north to escape the lingering oppression. Many settled in America's largest cities, such as New York and Chicago.

ROCKEFELLER, CARNEGIE, AND MELLON

Titans of Business

By the late nineteenth century, the American economy was expanding in all directions. Enormous fortunes were accumulated, often by men who skirted the law or were ruthless in their business practices. They sought to allay public anger by making large charitable donations and founding institutions of learning. Three of the most important of these nineteenth-century power brokers were John D. Rockefeller Sr., Andrew Carnegie, and Andrew Mellon.

THE ROCKEFELLER DYNASTY

John D. Rockefeller Sr. made his fortune with the Standard Oil Company, formed in 1870. During the 1880s, Rockefeller's Standard Oil Trust controlled virtually all of the nation's refineries. Not surprisingly, antitrust sentiments prevailed, and as the trust dissolved, Rockefeller formed Standard Oil of New Jersey as a holding company until the Supreme Court broke it up in 1911. Rockefeller retired early, his personal wealth a staggering $1 billion—and this was before income tax existed!

Upon his father's retirement in 1911, John D. Rockefeller Jr. assumed the reins in business. He also led the board of directors of the Rockefeller Foundation (among other board posts), and in 1930, he began supervising a massive undertaking in New York City. It was an extensive complex of buildings, completed in 1939, known as Rockefeller Center, where the ice rink and Christmas celebrations remain prominent today. Rockefeller's philanthropy extended also to New York City land given to the United Nations (upon which the international headquarters was established) and to the restoration of Colonial Williamsburg in Virginia.

American Castles

To express their wealth, America's millionaires (and billionaires) built gigantic houses for themselves and their families. Among the most prominent are:

- The Breakers in Newport, Rhode Island, a seventy-room mansion built by Cornelius Vanderbilt II as a summer home
- Marble House in Newport, a fifty-room summer home of Alva and William Vanderbilt
- Kykuit, John D. Rockefeller's retreat in Westchester County, New York, a mere forty rooms
- The Henry Clay Frick House, located on Fifth Avenue in New York City, now an art museum

ANDREW CARNEGIE

While John Rockefeller Sr. and his family retained a reputation for brutally crushing labor opposition, Andrew Carnegie is traditionally portrayed as the epitome of a "good capitalist." Carnegie was born in Scotland in 1835 to poor parents and immigrated to the United States when he was thirteen. Through hard work and a painfully acquired education, Carnegie began to rise through the ranks of the Pennsylvania Railroad Company.

Both Carnegie and the company benefited considerably from the Civil War, in which railroads were key as a means of transporting troops and supplies. After the war, Carnegie turned his energies to the construction trade, though he retained his railway connections. The period of post-war rebuilding required vast amounts of iron, and Carnegie's company was able to supply this and to secure many construction contracts, the foundation of his large fortune.

Forged from Steel

Carnegie's plants manufactured Bessemer steel, a new way of forging the metal from pig iron. In 1901 J. Pierpont Morgan bought out Carnegie and formed the United States Steel Corporation, the first corporation with a capitalization of more than $1 billion.

Among the philanthropic projects Carnegie undertook were:

- A series of Carnegie libraries, both in Britain and in the United States
- The Carnegie Institute of Technology in Pittsburgh (later Carnegie-Mellon University)
- Carnegie Hall in New York City
- A pension fund for college professors that later evolved into TIAA-CREF (Teachers Insurance and Annuity Association–College Retirement Equities Fund)

ANDREW MELLON

Unlike Carnegie and Rockefeller, who, though active in political circles, remained free of political office, Andrew Mellon became secretary of the treasury in the administrations of Warren Harding, Calvin Coolidge, and Herbert Hoover.

The source of his wealth was his financial abilities, which were considerable, and in manufacturing, using aluminum, steel, and coke (a type of slow-burning fuel). As secretary of the treasury, his main goal was to cut income tax, particularly on the top layers of the population. He argued (as would later economists during the administration of Ronald Reagan) that reducing taxes would lead wealthy people to invest more in the economy, creating more wealth. This sort of theory became harder to sustain with the onset of the Great Depression in 1929.

Liquidate! Liquidate!

During the Depression, Mellon advocated harsh measures to get the economy moving again. "Liquidate labor, liquidate stocks, liquidate farmers, liquidate real estate," he urged Herbert Hoover. "It will purge the rottenness out of the system."

Rockefeller, Carnegie, and Mellon typify a new upper class in the United States, one whose wealth was founded not on land, but on factories and mills. The new industrial age had come to America.

BUSTING THE TRUSTS

Reforming Capitalism

When William McKinley was assassinated in 1901, Theodore Roosevelt became the youngest president at the age of forty-two. Full of energy and idealism, Roosevelt was well traveled and well read and loved strenuous exercise of all kinds. Raised in a wealthy family, he was also well connected, knowing many prominent business leaders. His image as a fairly ordinary citizen enhanced his appeal, and in turn, he often championed the causes of the working class.

TEDDY ROOSEVELT, THE TRUSTBUSTER

When coal miners in Pennsylvania went on strike for higher wages in 1902, President Roosevelt threatened to seize the mines if owners would not agree to arbitration. Similar actions earned him the moniker of "Trustbuster" when he acted to stop unfair practices in the big businesses of tobacco, oil, steel, and the railroads. These industries had established trusts, working together to limit competition. The most famous was the Standard Oil Trust run by John D. Rockefeller.

Roosevelt's reform efforts sparked great political opposition. In February 1902, Roosevelt brought suit under the Sherman Antitrust Act against the railroad trust of the Northern Securities Company. The people loved him for it, and when the case went before the Supreme Court, the decision came in five to four against the trust. Actually, the president did not want to disband all of these trusts—just the most flagrant ones. He called his moderate approach the "Square Deal."

Antitrust

The Sherman Antitrust Act of 1890 regulated the operations of corporate trusts and declared that every contract, combination in the form of trust, or other act in restraint of trade was illegal.

THE BULL MOOSE PARTY

In 1912, Roosevelt, angry at the policies of his successor, William Howard Taft, decided to run again for president. When he was defeated in the Republican primaries, he broke off from the party and formed a new organization: the Progressive Party. This party quickly became known as the Bull Moose Party (Roosevelt had told reporters he was "fit as a bull moose"). The party nominated Roosevelt for president, and he ran against Taft and the Democratic candidate, Woodrow Wilson. Because Roosevelt and Taft split the Republican vote, Wilson won the election, and Roosevelt largely retired from politics.

The River of Doubt

In 1914, after losing a third-party run for the presidency, Roosevelt traveled to Latin America. There, in collaboration with the great explorer Cândido Rondon, he undertook to trace the course of a previously unmapped river, the Rio da Dúvida, or "River of Doubt." Today, this river is known as Rio Roosevelt.

ORGANIZED LABOR

The Union's Inspiration

Large factories had become the major employers for most people—a result of the Industrial Revolution at the end of the eighteenth century. But the downside to that was that workers lacked protection from almost all contingencies, including inflation, illness, disability, and arbitrary firing. Workers soon banded together, demanding a voice and a change in labor conditions. The 1870s were marked with particular unrest given the sad state of the nation's economy in 1873. A secret fraternal order called the Knights of Labor embraced workers in many occupations, becoming one of the most powerful early unions. In 1881, workers met in Columbus, Ohio, to establish a far more effective group called the American Federation of Labor (AFL). Its first leader was Samuel Gompers, president of the Cigar Makers' International Union and of the Federation of Organized Trades and Labor Unions. The AFL gave workers more rights, such as negotiating with employers for better conditions and wages.

Early American Unions

Among the labor organizations of nineteenth-century America were the National Labor Union (founded 1866), the American Railway Union (founded 1893), and the Knights of Labor (founded 1870).

Several disastrous strikes, coupled with the depression of this era, stunted union growth. In 1892, large numbers of private detectives as well as National Guard troops quelled striking workers at

Carnegie Steel Company's Homestead Mill in Pittsburgh, essentially destroying the union. In 1894, a strike by the American Railway Union against the Pullman Company was defeated by an injunction issued under the Sherman Antitrust Act.

But after the Spanish-American War, the trade union movement grew, so that by 1904, more than 2 million workers belonged to trade unions. Almost 1.7 million joined the AFL. With great reluctance, employers gradually accepted collective bargaining with the unions as the norm.

"Solidarity Forever"

Perhaps the most famous union anthem, "Solidarity Forever" was written by Ralph Chaplin in 1915:

> When the union's inspiration through the workers' blood shall run
> There can be no power greater anywhere beneath the sun
> Yet what force on earth is weaker than the feeble strength of one?
> But the union makes us strong!

Presidents in the last quarter of the nineteenth century typically sided with business owners against workers who went out on strike with their grievances. Sensing new public sentiment, Roosevelt sent in federal troops to a Pennsylvania mine strike, not only to protect the mines themselves, but to protect the strikers as well. Business owners were known to hire thugs to beat up striking workers, and the presence of soldiers prevented violence and led to more peaceful resolution of labor/management disputes.

THE HAYMARKET AFFAIR

In the late spring of 1886, workers in Chicago launched a strike demanding an eight-hour workday. They were joined by workers in other cities, including New York, Detroit, and Milwaukee. Many of the workers were immigrants, accustomed to working shifts as long as fourteen or fifteen hours.

Tension grew between the striking workers and strikebreakers hired by companies such as the McCormick machine company. On May 3, during a rally outside the plant, violence broke out; police fired into the crowd, killing several of the strikers.

Leaders of the strike, including the anarchist August Spies, called for a rally the following day at Haymarket Square. The meeting was peaceful until about 10:30 P.M., when a large group of police entered the square and commanded the crowd to disperse. At that point someone—it has never been established who—threw a bomb at the police. It exploded, killing seven policemen. The police responded with gunfire, killing at least one demonstrator.

Despite a lack of evidence that he had anything to do with the bomb, Spies was arrested and charged with murder. As well, seven other known anarchists were arrested and charged with murder—although only two of them were actually in the square when the bomb was thrown. In the hysterical atmosphere that swept the city in the aftermath of the bombing, all eight defendants were convicted and four, including Spies, were hanged.

THE AUTOMOBILE

America on Wheels

No invention did more to transform the face of America, both culturally and physically, than the automobile. Although the modern car was invented by a German, Karl Benz, its development has been inextricably linked to American history in the late nineteenth and early twentieth centuries.

The first commercial American cars were built in Massachusetts by the Duryea brothers in the 1890s. By the turn of the century, some of the familiar names—Studebaker, Daimler, Diesel—were turning out automobiles. The real breakthrough came in 1902 with the invention of mass production.

HENRY FORD AND THE MODEL T

Henry Ford, contrary to popular thought, didn't invent the assembly line. In America, the first assembly line was built by Ransom E. Olds in 1902. What Ford did was to substantially improve it and expand its capacity to produce cars quickly. Ford divided the assembly of the car into a series of different, discrete tasks that could be performed by workers remaining in a single spot on the line. This saved time and improved safety. The result was that a Ford could be built in approximately fifteen minutes.

Ford also realized that there was no point in making cars fast if no one could afford them. He kept his products cheap, well within the affordability of the growing American middle class. One of his workers could buy a car with four months' pay.

Ford and Anti-Semitism

In addition to his role as an industrial leader and innovator, Henry Ford was, unfortunately, an active anti-Semite. *The Dearborn Independent*, a newspaper that Ford backed, was strongly anti-Jewish. Ford also published and circulated the forgery known as *The Protocols of the Elders of Zion*, an anti-Semitic tract invented by the Russian secret police.

Beginning in 1908, the Ford Motor Company began producing the Model T, which became the most popular car in the United States. In today's dollars, it cost consumers about $7,500. In all, more than 15 million Model Ts were produced.

"Any Color As Long As It's Black"

Legend (perpetuated by Ford himself) says that Ford told buyers they could only get the Model T in black. In fact this wasn't true; Model Ts were produced in other colors, including red.

AMERICA ON WHEELS

Possessing a car meant that a family's range of travel widened tremendously. American families took vacations together, traveling across the country in their cars. A whole range of services and industries rose up to meet this new product. The American landscape became dotted with gas stations, garages, and motels.

Houses were increasingly built with garages in which to store the family car. By the 1950s, the garage door facing the street had become many houses' most prominent feature. The car became a status symbol; at first it was enough to own one, but as time went on people were judged by the *kind* of car they owned.

Detroit, center of the automobile industry, grew rapidly, with giant plants such as the Ford River Rouge Complex, finished in 1928. In the 1930s, more than 100,000 people worked at the plant.

In 1956, Congress authorized the construction of the Interstate Highway System, one of the most massive engineering projects in the history of the United States. Completed thirty-five years later (and expanded again in 2012), it added more than 47,000 miles of paved road to the United States, making travel even easier for an increasingly car-centric society.

WORLD WAR I

Mr. Wilson's War

The son of a Presbyterian minister, Woodrow Wilson took the oath of office in 1913 determined to live up to his new commitment. Indeed, his high moral principles were tested, for it took much skill to keep the United States at peace in a world moving toward war. World War I (also known as "the War to End All Wars," and "the Great War") raged in Europe from 1914 to 1918, and resulted in the end of the Austro-Hungarian, German, Ottoman, and Russian Empires.

MAIN POWERS FIGHTING IN WORLD WAR I

Allies
- United Kingdom
- France
- Russia
- Japan
- United States

Central Powers
- Germany
- Austro-Hungary
- Ottoman Empire
- Bulgaria

ASSASSINATION!

In June 1914, Austro-Hungarian archduke Franz Ferdinand and his wife were assassinated by Serbian nationalists as they rode through the streets of Sarajevo in Bosnia. This event, though it didn't lead immediately to conflict, provoked hostilities in Europe and fostered the combat readiness of many armies put on alert. These deep-rooted hostilities were remnants of political and economic struggles that had raged throughout Europe in the previous century. The assassination was not the sole trigger of international tensions, merely a catalyst. In August, the Austro-Hungarian Empire declared war on Serbia.

CAUSES OF THE GREAT WAR

The Great War occurred as a result of a series of interlocking treaties and alliances, many of which had been constructed during the past fifty years with the intention of *preventing* such a war. Key to it was the slow breakup of the Ottoman Empire (one diplomat referred to it as the "sick man of Europe") and the scramble for imperial possessions by other countries.

In the Balkan Peninsula, the various small states such as Serbia, Bosnia, and Macedonia sought the protection of larger powers. When Franz Ferdinand was assassinated, Russia feared that Austria would use the event as an excuse to annex Serbia. Germany, as a result of its treaty of alliance, backed Austria-Hungary. On July 28, 1914, Austria declared war on Serbia, and this caused Russia, an ally of Serbia, to mobilize. Germany sent an ultimatum to Russia to halt its mobilization or face German action. Russia refused, and Germany then declared war on Russia on August 1. France, a Russian ally, wanted to regain the Alsace-Lorraine region, which it had lost to Germany in the Franco-Prussian War of 1870–71. Germany declared war on France on August 3, and also invaded Luxembourg and Belgium. Britain, France's ally, was now drawn into the conflict as well.

Cousin Versus Cousin

World War I was fought between countries whose rulers were relatives. King George V of England was the first cousin of Kaiser Wilhelm of Germany and Czar Nicholas II of Russia. Queen Victoria, grandmother to these royal children, had been their determined matchmaker, believing that if she arranged international marriages it would help bring about world peace.

CONFLICT SPREADS

In the United States, President Wilson was committed to neutrality while the other countries began to fight. Britain's sea power had effectively halted German shipping, but this created problems for the United States, which had supplied food and arms to both sides. The British tightened their blockade, and as Germany's supply routes were closed off, the Germans faced starvation unless they worked around it. By April 1917 more than $2 billion worth of goods had been sold by the United States to England and the Allied countries. The German navy used submarines, called U-boats, to torpedo vessels supplying England. Unfortunately, this included U.S. ships.

SUBMARINES LET LOOSE

In April 1915, the British Cunard liner *Lusitania* prepared to leave New York harbor. While the German embassy had issued a warning to travelers to cross the Atlantic at their own risk, many gave little heed to that admonition. On May 7, the *Lusitania* was passing Ireland on its way to England when a German submarine attacked, sinking the ship with 1,198 passengers onboard, including 126 Americans. Germany insisted that the *Lusitania* carried munitions; the United States denied the allegations (though it would later be learned that there were shell casings, cartridges, and small-arms ammunition onboard). Even though the ship's sinking enraged Americans, who felt the Germans had attacked a defenseless civilian vessel, the Wilson administration was still determined to keep the country out of war.

Wilson won re-election in 1916 while the war in Europe raged on. The numbers of casualties mounted: in the Battle of the Somme, 1.25 million men on both sides were killed, wounded, or captured, and the Battle of Verdun resulted in 1 million French and German casualties.

U.S. ENTRY INTO THE WAR

Wilson warned the German command of the United States' strong opposition to unrestricted submarine warfare. Therefore, when Germany announced that, effective February 1, 1917, unrestricted submarine warfare would be launched on all shipping to Great Britain, the president had little choice but to break off diplomatic relations. In a speech before Congress, Wilson suggested that if American ships were attacked, he would be forced to act. Not heeding the U.S. signals, the Germans sent secret telegrams to Mexico promising an alliance in return for help in defeating the United States should it enter the war. The British intercepted a telegram from Arthur Zimmermann, the German foreign minister to Mexico, which encouraged Mexican attacks upon the United States, offering the return of Arizona, Texas, and New Mexico in exchange. When the Zimmermann telegram was published in the newspapers, with Wilson's blessings, public opinion supporting war against Germany increased dramatically. Newspaper headlines read, "Kill the Kaiser!"

Reds under the Bed

The Red Scare resulted in America's obsession with Communism following the Bolshevik Revolution in 1917. In 1919, the U.S. House of Representatives refused to seat Socialist representative from Wisconsin, Victor L. Berger, because of his socialism, German ancestry, and antiwar views. In the 1920s, Attorney General Palmer organized a series of raids on labor and socialist organizations, arresting and deporting many foreign-born radicals.

Undaunted, German U-boats torpedoed two American ships (the *Illinois* and the *City of Memphis*) on March 16, 1917, and Wilson asked Congress to declare war. "It is a fearful thing to lead this great peaceful people into war, into the most terrible and disastrous of all wars, civilization itself seeming to be in the balance," Wilson said. Most of the nation rallied behind him. The United States officially declared war on Germany on April 6, 1917.

THE UNITED STATES DEPLOYS ITS FORCES

General John Pershing was given command of American Expeditionary Forces in Europe. But unlike its allies, the United States had no large standing army to send overseas, nor was the nation equipped with planes, ships, and other military equipment. Major efforts outfitted the newly drafted troops. Thus, the first American troops arrived in France in June 1917—approximately 200,000 Americans in training. They were ill prepared for the fierce warfare they encountered, but they were rested and had enthusiasm on their side. Americans began learning about poison gas, hand grenades, and demolition. Trench warfare provided some basic protection against enemy fire, but not nearly enough. Enemy soldiers raided the trenches, killing unsuspecting soldiers, and the mud and dampness wreaked havoc on the soldiers' health. Penicillin and other antibiotics didn't exist, so even minor cuts were potentially lethal.

GERMANY MAKES PEACE ON ITS EASTERN FRONT

The tide was starting to turn against the Germans. They had failed to destroy the British navy through submarine warfare and began sustaining heavy losses in their U-boat fleet, around the same time the Allies' shipbuilding efforts increased.

In December 1917, the new revolutionary government in Russia signed a peace agreement with the Austro-German negotiators, essentially ending eastern-front fighting. The Russian Revolution had occurred after Czar Nicholas II abdicated in March. Withdrawal from the Great War was a cardinal point in Bolshevik policy.

On September 26, 1918, American and French troops launched the Meuse-Argonne offensive in an effort to cut off the Germans between the Meuse River and the Argonne Forest, and British forces

breached the Hindenburg line the next day. The Germans had fortified this line for four years, reinforcing bunkers with concrete and
turning towns into virtual forts.

No News Today

Neither the British nor the German press (including official dispatches) were
forthcoming in their reports of the war. The title of Erich Maria Remarque's
great novel, *Im Westen nichts Neues* (*All Quiet on the Western Front*) was taken
from a German army dispatch on a day when thousands of soldiers were dying
in the trench warfare of World War I.

VICTORY AT HAND

Despite the preparations by the Germans, the fresh supply of Allied
troops, combined with overhead fighting power, overwhelmed them.
It took much forward movement and military strategy on land, in the
air, and through naval blockade, but the Hindenburg line was broken
on October 5, sealing Allied supremacy. The Allies were gaining on
the enemy. By November 1918, the American Expeditionary Forces
numbered nearly 2 million. On November 11, 1918, Germany and the
Allies reached an armistice agreement, thus ending years of heavy
fighting and world rancor.

THE END OF THE WAR

Many of those who'd survived the war died of influenza, as a worldwide epidemic struck. But victory was at hand. From January through

June of 1919, the Allies discussed the treaty, which came to be known as the Treaty of Versailles. Members of the Big Four—Georges Clemenceau of France, Vittorio Orlando of Italy, David Lloyd George of Britain, and Woodrow Wilson of the United States—met in the Hall of Mirrors at the French palace.

One provision of the Treaty of Versailles was the formation of a League of Nations, based on President Wilson's ideas for achieving lasting peace and world justice. However, for the League of Nations to truly effect peace, it required all members' assistance. If some withheld their cooperation, the league had no way of enforcing its will.

Over time, the League of Nations would observe the world stage as Germany rekindled the flames of another conflict. Even worse, the United States Senate didn't ratify the treaty, and the United States didn't join the League of Nations—this alone guaranteed the League's failure.

WOODROW WILSON'S FOURTEEN POINTS

The Fourteen Points was the name given to the proposals of President Woodrow Wilson to establish a lasting peace following the Allied victory in World War I. Wilson outlined these points in his address to a joint session of Congress in January 1918, giving further evidence of his moral leadership. Wilson's fourteen points included:

1. Peace agreements, openly arrived at, and abolition of secret diplomacy

2. Freedom of the seas in peace and war, except as the seas may be closed in whole or part by international action for enforcement of international covenants
3. Removal of international trade barriers wherever possible and establishment of an equality of trade conditions among the nations consenting to the peace
4. Reduction of armaments consistent with public safety
5. Adjustment of colonial disputes consistent with the interests of both the controlling government and the colonial population
6. Evacuation of Russian territory, with the proviso of self-determination
7. Evacuation and restoration of Belgium
8. Evacuation and restoration of French territory, including Alsace-Lorraine
9. Readjustment of Italian frontiers along clearly recognizable lines of nationality
10. Autonomy for the peoples of Austria-Hungary
11. Evacuation and restoration of territory to the Balkan nations
12. Self-determination for non-Turkish peoples under Turkish control and internationalization of the Dardanelles
13. An independent Poland, with access to the sea
14. Creation of a general association of nations

In order to secure support for his plan to create an association of nations, the president abandoned his insistence on accepting the full program. It was perhaps no surprise that Wilson's plan was ridiculed to some extent; Clemenceau commented that "the good Lord had only ten" points to make while Wilson insisted on more.

THE ROARING TWENTIES

Flappers and Bootleggers

As the 1920s began, Warren G. Harding took over the presidency after campaigning to return America to normalcy. On November 2, 1920, radio station KDKA in Pittsburgh broadcast the presidential election results. This spawned not only a new industry, but also a new way to disseminate news about the nation, its leaders, and its current events. Harding was the first president to address the nation using this new medium.

In keeping with his promise, Harding was a hands-off president who delegated much authority. Unfortunately, his trusted advisors became involved in numerous scandals. Before Harding could be impeached for any wrongdoing, he died in office in 1923, amid speculation of foul play.

Teapot Dome

The Teapot Dome scandal, named after an oil field in Wyoming, involved United States Secretary of the Interior Albert B. Fall leasing the rights to public oil fields to private oil companies (without competitive bidding) in exchange for thousands of dollars. Fall was found guilty and sentenced to one year in prison, making him the first cabinet member to go to jail for his actions while in office.

"THE BUSINESS OF AMERICA IS BUSINESS"

No president more embodied the idea that American government should promote the interests of business than Calvin Coolidge, whose administration lasted from 1923 to 1929. Coolidge did everything in his power to increase the profits taken in by business, arguing that what was good for capitalism in America was good for the country.

Like his secretary of the treasury, Andrew Carnegie, Coolidge believed that lower taxes would lead to greater prosperity and thus, ultimately, to higher tax revenues. Further, he argued, any restrictions on business by government simply got in the way of companies making money. So restraints of any kind were off, and the decade roared ahead.

WILD TIMES

The Roaring Twenties got their name from the outrageousness of the times. Prohibition, the outlawing of alcoholic beverages, restricted many people's lifestyles, tempting them to disobey the law. Illegal "speakeasy" bars flourished along with gangsters and organized crime.

The mindsets of many also changed. Cultural influences originated at the movies, in the work of well-known writers, and on Broadway. The 1920s served as the golden era for New York theater, which in prior decades had consisted of farces, melodramas, and musicals, but nothing of much literary merit. The Roaring Twenties spawned playwrights such as Eugene O'Neill and Noël Coward who dealt with serious social issues as well as farce. Also, a new style of music hit the nation, combining African-American folk rhythms with popular and European music. W.C. Handy, a black musician, was unable to attract a music publisher for his song "St. Louis Blues," so he published it himself in 1914. Forever after, his sound was known as jazz.

The Jazz Era, which many say first took hold in New Orleans, flourished with talented musicians such as Louis Armstrong. As African Americans migrated north for better industrial jobs, jazz caught hold in Chicago and in Harlem, a section of New York City that was undergoing its own renaissance.

Harlem Renaissance

This cultural movement, which lasted from about 1918 into the thirties, saw a flowering of African-American music, dance, theater, and literature, centered in the New York City neighborhood of Harlem on the upper East Side. Among those associated with it were:

- Duke Ellington (musician)
- Fats Waller (musician)
- Zora Neale Hurston (writer)
- Langston Hughes (writer)
- Josephine Baker (dancer)
- Paul Robeson (actor)

THE RADIO

In 1925, WSM Radio in Nashville, Tennessee, began airing barn dance music, which would later become known as the Grand Ole

Opry. In 1927, Congress expanded the Radio Act of 1912 to reflect this new industry, no longer run by amateurs but by commercial enterprises. Later, in 1934, it would be revised again with the creation of the Federal Communications Commission (FCC) to consider license applications and renewals for radio stations. The FCC also set guidelines for obscenity and false claims in advertising.

Prohibition

For years the Anti-Saloon League of America (ASL) had urged saloonkeepers to give up their businesses. By 1900, millions of men and women regarded drinking alcoholic beverages as a dangerous threat to families and society. On December 22, 1917, Congress submitted to the states the Eighteenth Amendment, which prohibited "the manufacture, sale, or transportation of intoxicating liquors." By January 1919, ratification was complete.

A TEST OF THE CONSTITUTION

The 1925 trial of a biology teacher named John Scopes, who had been arrested for teaching theories of evolution that contradicted the biblical version of creation, was another famous broadcasting moment. In his state of Tennessee, the law banned teaching any information that conflicted with the biblical account. Those who could not travel to the town of Dayton, Tennessee, could listen to the live broadcast. The American Civil Liberties Union (ACLU) named defense lawyer Clarence Darrow to represent Scopes in the carnival-like atmosphere that the trial created.

Former secretary of state William Jennings Bryan led the battle for the fundamentalists. Whether Scopes received a fair trial (a prayer opened each court session, and expert evolutionists were banned from taking the stand) is unclear. Scopes was found guilty, but was fined only $100. The Tennessee Supreme Court later overturned the local court's decision, citing a technicality. Although it never reached the U.S. Supreme Court, the Scopes trial served to showcase many freedoms in the Bill of Rights—the freedoms of speech, religion, and the separation of church and state.

IMMIGRATION POLICIES ARE TIGHTENED

The Immigration Act of 1924 became another controversial political issue stemming from the Red Scare, for it set quotas on the number of immigrants allowed into the United States. Many in the mass wave of immigration originated from southern and eastern European countries. The American labor unions became concerned that continued immigration would threaten their jobs. Congress responded by passing the act, which limited immigration to 2 percent of each nationality present in the United States in the year 1880. This year was chosen mainly because at that time there were very few people of Far Eastern and East European descent present in the United States, thus severely limiting further influx.

This was a turning point for the country. No longer were the huddled masses ensured a home in America. Years later, the Immigration and Naturalization Act of 1965 put an end to national quotas for immigration, making individual talents and skills or close relationships with U.S. citizens a better basis for admittance.

CRASH!

The Great Depression

Throughout the 1920s, Americans speculated in stocks in record numbers. When they didn't have the disposable cash, they invested their life savings as well as borrowed money. Those who were highly leveraged lost everything when market jitters began on October 24, 1929. The massive selling spree of millions of shares collapsed businesses and sent investors and brokers scrambling. On October 29, 1929, the market hit bottom. On this "Black Tuesday," the single worst day for the New York Stock Exchange, hotel clerks reportedly asked patrons checking in if they required a room for sleeping or jumping. It used to be thought that the stock market collapse caused the Great Depression, but there were several causes:

1. The economy was growing at a rate that was far too fast to sustain.
2. Increased industrialization and wealth remained in the hands of a few. Too many products chased consumers who couldn't possibly purchase all of them.
3. Workers lost their jobs when industry cut back, and the spiraling effect began.
4. During Prohibition, bootlegging made money for organized crime figures and even respectable businessmen, but it did little for the national economy.
5. For nearly a century, single-crop farming had ruined the soil and contributed to cycles of drought and flooding in America's farm belt.

HOOVER TRIES TO WAIT IT OUT

Herbert Hoover seemed to be the best person for the challenging job of dragging America's economy back from the brink. The once-orphaned Hoover was a self-made businessman and a millionaire, and plenty of voters saw him as the quintessential American success story. Hoover had even distributed food as Wilson's national food administrator in World War I. But as the effects of the Depression deepened, many unfairly blamed Hoover and lost faith in his policies of economic isolationism.

Government Assistance

Other nations, such as Great Britain, were reaching out to the poor with payments to the unemployed and the elderly. Most Americans began to believe that their own government owed them some form of assistance. But President Hoover, though sympathetic, held fast to his principle of individual responsibility.

Clearly, Hoover failed to grasp the extent and severity of the problem. When in March 1930 he claimed that the worst was just about over, the unemployment rate rose, more businesses failed, banks closed, and many people defaulted on their mortgages and lost their homes. Congress tried to respond to the economic crisis with the Smoot-Hawley Tariff Act of 1930 that raised tariff rates to record levels. Although hesitant to put his name on the legislation, President Hoover signed it anyway. The intention was to increase sales of U.S. products by raising the cost of imported goods, but the measure was a miserable failure. An international trade war broke out, drastically reducing overseas sales of U.S.-made goods. As international trade weakened, foreign countries plunged into what was now a worldwide depression.

THE CRISIS DEEPENS

By 1932, approximately 12 million people were out of work compared to 4 million two years before. Soup and bread lines were common sights. Schools had to close when they couldn't afford their operating costs, forcing many teachers out of work and creating an educational void for many children. Because of the president's lack of government assistance, his name was given to the growing wretched shantytowns—called "Hoovervilles"—while those who had only newspaper to protect them from the cold were said to use "Hoover blankets." The president once hailed for his humanitarian gestures was now ridiculed for his failure to help the American people.

Words of Wisdom

"Economic depression cannot be cured by legislative action or executive pronouncement."
—Herbert Hoover

The events in Washington, D.C., in May 1932 made matters worse. Thousands of World War I veterans, once promised a bonus from the army, walked, rode the rails, or otherwise made their way to the nation's capital to demand the payment, which they needed immediately, not in the mid-1940s when the payments were scheduled to occur. Congress turned them down, and some members of the "Bonus Army" disbanded while others persevered. That July, Hoover lost patience with the contingent of former soldiers and ordered the standing U.S. Army, led by General Douglas MacArthur, to drive them away with tear gas. Once again, Hoover demonstrated insensitivity to the people's plight.

VOTES FOR WOMEN

Weaker Sex No Longer

Women's rights in the 1800s were very limited—husbands had the legal right to exercise total authority over their wives. Married women couldn't retain their own wages, control their own property, or even keep custody of their children if they sought a divorce. During the late nineteenth century, states began to gradually recognize women's rights. In the prosperous postwar era, women stashed conservative clothing in their closets and wore dresses that clung to their bodies and skirts above the knee. Such fashionable women became known as "flappers." They cut their hair shorter in a "bobbed" style and enjoyed a new sense of freedom not granted to prior generations of young ladies. These women were the first to openly smoke and the first to dance "wildly." Women also began to enter careers beyond the limits of nursing or teaching, for typewriting skills yielded further job prospects for millions of women—far more than worked around the turn of the century.

Emma Willard, self-taught in algebra, geometry, geography, and history, tutored young ladies and petitioned the New York legislature to open a girl's school. She didn't stop there, though; her strides led to female teachers, more competitive salaries, and financing for women's education.

Elizabeth Cady Stanton began crusading as an abolitionist, but her work furthered women's rights as well. Stanton joined Lucretia Coffin Mott, Lucy Stone, and Susan B. Anthony in speaking out in favor of a woman's right to vote, a right once granted by some colonies in Colonial America but lost years later. Carrie Chapman Catt proved to be a talented organizer and served as president of the National American Woman Suffrage Association. These women reformers became known as *suffragists*, and the American suffragist movement scored its major achievement following the victory in World War I. In 1919, Congress approved the Nineteenth Amendment providing that "the right of citizens of the United States to vote shall not be denied or abridged by the United States or by any State on account of sex." The amendment was ratified August 18, 1920.

Famous American Women

Women who had tremendous impact throughout American history include:

- Frances Perkins, the first female cabinet member as secretary of labor during Franklin D. Roosevelt's administration
- Jeannette Rankin, the first woman to serve in Congress
- Susan B. Anthony, tireless crusader for votes for women
- Sandra Day O'Connor, the first female Supreme Court justice
- Sally Ride, the first American woman in space
- Shirley Chisholm, the first African-American woman to serve in Congress

Another important effort benefiting women was Margaret Sanger's crusade for contraceptives and the newly coined phrase "birth control." As a nurse in some of the poorer sections of New York City, Sanger saw women overburdened with more children than they could care for. She believed that oversized families spawned poverty, and that in any case, women should have rights over their own bodies. Sanger opened the country's first birth control clinic in Brooklyn in 1916, but those who viewed her activities and the information she disseminated as obscene thwarted her efforts. But Sanger wasn't deterred easily, and in 1952, she persuaded a friend to back research that ultimately led to "the pill," or oral contraceptives. However, not until 1965 did the U.S. Supreme Court invalidate laws banning the dissemination of birth control information and prescriptions.

THE NEW DEAL

Defeating Fear Itself

Facing the 1932 election, the Republicans renominated Hoover as their candidate. The Democrats chose Franklin Delano Roosevelt, who had first earned a seat in Congress from New York in 1910 as a liberal Democrat.

Once elected, FDR implemented sweeping changes through government programs aimed at alleviating the misery of the Great Depression. On inauguration day, many states had declared bank holidays in order to keep the remaining banks solvent. They feared the runs on the banking system that had already occurred with depositors lining up to withdraw their money.

Words of Wisdom

"So, first of all, let me assert my firm belief that the only thing we have to fear is fear itself—nameless, unreasoning, unjustified terror which paralyzes needed efforts to convert retreat into advance."
—Franklin Roosevelt

Two days later, on March 6, President Roosevelt called a halt to banking operations, and three days later Congress, which had been called to special session, passed the Emergency Banking Act of 1933. Federal auditors examined bankbooks, and the president's first "fireside chat" renewed trust in the banking system. As the president explained, unsound banks would be closed. Approximately 12,000 banks were back in business.

Roosevelt followed up with massive reform as Congress established the Federal Deposit Insurance Corporation (FDIC) in 1933, which guaranteed individual deposits up to $5,000 (that amount has increased over time). The new law, just as the president had intended, gave investors the confidence that if the bank failed, they wouldn't lose all their funds. Two acts, one in 1933 and another the following year, brought forth detailed regulations for the securities market, enforced by the newly created Securities and Exchange Commission (SEC). Joseph P. Kennedy (father of the future president) became the commission's first chairman.

The End of Prohibition

In November 1933, the Twenty-first Amendment repealed Prohibition. Most Americans heralded its passage (though the state of Utah was the last to ratify it). In the decade prior, Prohibition had led to bootlegging, smuggling, and an increase in organized crime. In addition, the economic crisis created a demand for federal revenues from the taxation of alcohol.

ACRONYMS FOR THE PEOPLE

As the administration unveiled its New Deal programs, it appeared as an alphabet soup of projects, for many of the initiatives were identified by acronyms. For instance:

- The Federal Housing Administration (FHA) offered loan guarantees for home purchases.
- The Civilian Conservation Corps (CCC) aided the unemployed by giving jobs to men between eighteen and twenty-five and

putting them to work in rural camps built by the War Department (today's Department of Defense). These young men planted trees, built dams, and provided other services that conserved the environment.

- The Federal Emergency Relief Administration (FERA) was created in 1933 and led by Roosevelt's trusted advisor Harry Hopkins. FERA made initial cash payments to the unemployed, but also put people to work in jobs that didn't compete with private enterprise.
- The Agricultural Adjustment Act (AAA) was a complex farm bill that paid farmers to take land out of cultivation. At a time when the needy often lacked food, this bill invited intense criticism. It had been intended to raise agricultural prices, but in 1936 it **was** declared unconstitutional by the U.S. Supreme Court.

SOCIAL SECURITY

One of the most important New Deal programs stemmed from passage of the Social Security Act on August 14, 1935. This legislation consisted of three core components—a retirement fund for the elderly, unemployment insurance, and welfare grants for local distribution (which included aid for dependent children). Social Security was developed in the United States later than in several European countries, which had instituted such programs before World War I. Two years after the Social Security program was passed into law, 21 million workers were covered by unemployment insurance and 36 million were entitled to old-age pensions.

THE TENNESSEE VALLEY AUTHORITY

The Tennessee Valley Authority (TVA) was particularly innovative, building dams in seven southeastern states to generate electricity and manage flood control programs. Power came to thousands in rural regions where electricity had not previously been delivered. Perhaps the cornerstone of the New Deal was the National Industrial Recovery Act passed in 1933 to establish the National Recovery Administration (NRA). It was supposed to encourage good business by establishing codes of fair competition. Workers were guaranteed such things as minimum wages, maximum hours, and the right to collective bargaining.

Unfortunately, the NRA didn't work as its supporters had anticipated. Its director, the former army officer Hugh S. Johnson, resigned after failing to win over the American people, and in 1935, the Supreme Court declared the NRA unconstitutional.

THE NEW DEAL AND THE NATION

The New Deal seemed to be off to a rousing start; in the first hundred days of the new administration there was a flurry of legislation to get the country moving forward again. Public works projects put thousands on the job, creating infrastructure such as the Lincoln Tunnel connecting New York with New Jersey, as well as the Golden Gate Bridge in San Francisco. Whatever political opposition the president faced was taken care of in 1934 when Democrats swept the midterm elections, increasing their majorities in both the Senate and the House.

FRANKLIN D. ROOSEVELT

The Patrician Reformer

Franklin Roosevelt was an unlikely agent of social change. He was born into aristocracy in 1882; the Roosevelts were among the most important families in New York and in the country. FDR grew up in an atmosphere of wealth and privilege.

The cousin of former president Theodore Roosevelt, he attended a prominent prep school and then Harvard. He became a lawyer and seemed headed for a distinguished career representing corporations.

Eleanor Roosevelt

In 1905, FDR married his cousin Eleanor, daughter of Elliot Roosevelt, who was Theodore Roosevelt's brother. Although Eleanor was shy, during her husband's presidency and afterward she became one of the most outspoken advocates on behalf of the poor and displaced in the United States.

FDR began his political career in the New York state senate. Through his hard work and his family connections, he rose rapidly, becoming assistant secretary of the navy in the Wilson administration. As early as 1907, he was being spoken of as a possible presidential candidate. However, he was crippled by polio in 1921 and sidelined his political aspirations during his rehabilitation. Roosevelt bought property in Warm Springs, Georgia, where he worked to improve his health and the health of others, mostly children whom he flew to the resortlike atmosphere for their own rehabilitation. Though he made progress with his recovery, Roosevelt would forever be confined to a wheelchair (however, since it was before the advent of television, most Americans were not aware of this). The public rarely saw him sitting in a wheelchair or using the steel braces he needed to walk. By common, unspoken consent, the press almost never photographed Roosevelt while he was in motion.

FDR's polio struggle transformed this wealthy New Yorker into a champion of the poor and downtrodden. At several important junctures he broke from his own capitalist class to side with labor or others with interests contrary to those of the wealthy. That transformation served him well. Roosevelt's campaign slogan stated "Happy Days Are Here Again," and he won the election.

The Court-Packing Fiasco

Frustrated with the series of Supreme Court decisions that ruled large swaths of the New Deal unconstitutional, in 1937 Roosevelt made an attempt to expand membership in the court. He proposed that for each justice who reached the age of seventy-and-a-half, the president should be entitled to appoint one additional justice, up to fifteen. After heated debate, the measure was defeated in Congress.

Even with the progress of Roosevelt's first hundred days, the work of restoring the economy was by no means finished. Other New Deal measures included the Wealth Tax, which raised individual income tax rates for some, as well as the federal Fair Labor Standards Act of 1938, mandating maximum hours and minimum wages for most workers. In addition, the Works Progress Administration (WPA) provided government funding not only for building construction, but also for artists and writers. As a result, murals were painted, plays performed, photographs taken, and folk music sung. Through the Federal Writers' Project, state-by-state guidebooks were created, while the Federal Theater Project staged free performances.

Though the New Deal failed to stimulate comprehensive economic recovery, it set the nation on its course with increased controls over the money supply and Federal Reserve policies. Even more importantly, it gave everyone a better understanding of the economic consequences of taxation, debt, and spending. This knowledge helped the federal government to limit the impact of later recessions. A number of the agencies created then still exist today.

THE NEWSWORTHY AND NOTABLE

Roosevelt's Brain Trust was instrumental in the passage of his unprecedented array of social programs. The individuals forming this advisory group consisted of government outsiders, including professors, lawyers, and economic experts. The enduring legacy of the New Deal was government's increased involvement in the lives of its citizens.

Among the prominent members of the Brain Trust were:

- Felix Frankfurter
- Frances Perkins
- Harry Hopkins
- Harold Ickes
- Louis Brandeis
- Thomas Corcoran

WORLD WAR II

Freedom in the Balance

The end of World War I left the world in an unstable condition. The Treaty of Versailles had disarmed the German military and replaced the kaiser with a democratic government, for which Germany had no previous model. The League of Nations lacked the ability to act decisively. The financial crisis that began in 1929 shattered economies across the globe. The Russian Revolution popularized communism and strengthened revolutionary parties in other countries. As if that weren't enough, fascism was gaining influence in many countries, but particularly in Italy.

GERMAN AND ITALIAN DISCONTENT

In Germany, the National Socialist German Workers' (Nazi) Party attracted a large following, appealing to anti-Semitism and attacking the German Communists and Socialists. By 1932, the Nazi Party wielded considerable power in the German parliament (called the Reichstag). German president Paul von Hindenburg was growing weak in his advanced years. Adolf Hitler, known for his racial hatred and contempt for democracy, took advantage of the situation and won a following that placed him in a position to ascend to power. Hitler gained the chancellorship in January 1933 and became dictator three months later. Before von Hindenburg's death, Hitler had already ordered the killings of high-ranking Germans whom he saw as a threat to his power. Books that contained thoughts contrary to the Nazi beliefs were burned.

The *Hindenburg* Crash

The *Hindenburg*, a German airship that began transatlantic passenger service in 1936, was a source of Nazi pride. But on May 6, 1937, as it approached Lakehurst, New Jersey, the dirigible burst into flames and crashed, killing many onboard and one person on the ground.

Under Hitler's leadership, Germany began to rearm, defying the Treaty of Versailles. Most Allies, along with the League of Nations, stood idly by as the new dictator seized control over the industrial heartland of the Ruhr. The prime minister and dictator of Italy, Benito Mussolini, was an ally of Hitler and also a Fascist. He invaded the country of Ethiopia.

Fascism in America

Hitler's obsession with creating a pure master race, free from Jewish influence, found support among some in the United States. Groups such as the Ku Klux Klan whipped up hatred for African Americans, many of whom had migrated north to big cities, seeking employment. The German American Bund held mass rallies in several major cities in support of Hitler.

Hitler's police force (called the Gestapo, a branch of the Schutzstaffel, or SS for short) began rounding up Jews and other supposed undesirables, who were then sent to forced labor camps. Those able to work were used to build roads or provide other manual labor, but the rest were exterminated in camps such as Auschwitz in Poland. Gas chambers, disguised as showers, killed millions. It wasn't immediately apparent that Hitler was systematically murdering Jews, but in time, Nazi atrocities were unveiled to the world's horror.

THE WORLD MAKES CONCESSIONS

Nazi Germany and Fascist Italy made their alliance formal in 1936 with the Rome-Berlin Axis. Meanwhile, the Empire of Japan aligned with Germany against Communism, and Italy followed suit. In 1938, Hitler invaded Austria, annexing it to his Third Reich. Not satisfied, he went after the Sudetenland in Czechoslovakia, demanding its annexation. The Treaty of Versailles had formed Czechoslovakia at the conclusion of World War I. France and Britain, based on the terms of a treaty, should have defended the Sudetenland, but to pacify Hitler and avoid conflict they didn't oppose his aggression. In fact, British Prime Minister Neville Chamberlain returned to Britain in 1938 with Hitler's signature on the Munich Pact, guaranteeing what Chamberlain called "peace in our time."

Proving he couldn't be trusted, one year later Hitler seized the rest of Czechoslovakia, followed by a portion of Lithuania. During this same period, Mussolini took Albania. The Treaty of Versailles had given part of German territory to Poland, an area known as the Polish Corridor. When Germany rolled tanks into the Polish Corridor with massive force on September 1, 1939, France and Britain could no longer watch from the sidelines. World War II erupted.

The Germans invited the Soviets into Poland from the east early that September, and by September 6, the Polish government fled Warsaw. Dividing Poland between Germany and Russia made it look as if there were an alliance between the two countries. Indeed, the Soviet Union and Germany had signed a nonaggression pact in 1939. However, Hitler had long desired to conquer the Soviet Union. The pact simply bought him some time.

The Spanish Civil War

While Germany declared war on the world, the Spanish Civil War erupted. Factions, one led by Generalissimo Francisco Franco, struggled from 1936 to 1939. Hitler and Mussolini aided Franco as if they were practicing for larger conflicts to come. Again, countries including the United States remained neutral. However, a number of Americans sympathetic to the cause of the Spanish Loyalists (that is, the anti-Francoists) traveled to Spain and fought alongside Spanish troops. Among those who went to Spain was the writer Ernest Hemingway, who traveled there as a reporter and later turned his experiences into the novel *For Whom the Bell Tolls,* the story of a young American who fought in the war.

FRANCE DIGS IN

The French held fast to the Maginot Line, a series of strong fortifications built in the 1930s along the Franco-German frontier to ensure that Germans stayed on their side. The line ran from Switzerland to the Belgium-Luxembourg border and into the south of France. At one end lay the Ardennes Forest.

Believing Hitler's army would attack through Belgium over the open plains (much as Germany had done in World War I), France and Britain mobilized to meet the German troops east of Brussels. Germany, however, chose to invade France through the Ardennes, cutting off the British and French armies in Belgium. The British, aiding their French allies, had to escape across the English Channel to avoid capture. But unlike the French, who gave in to German terms, the British vowed to fight on. Chamberlain, who had led Great Britain into its war effort, was forced to resign in May 1940. Sir Winston Churchill succeeded him and proved to be one of President Roosevelt's closest confidants during the crises ahead.

Former Naval Person

Although at this stage of the war the United States maintained its neutrality, Churchill and Roosevelt kept up an active correspondence. In a not-terribly-subtle effort at discretion, Churchill signed his letters to Roosevelt "Former naval person" (Churchill had been attached to the British Admiralty in World War I). The naval background of both men provided common ground for them to talk.

EUROPE IN DISTRESS

As America watched, the Royal Air Force in Great Britain was besieged by German air attacks. Terrified Londoners had crowded into underground subways for protection from the nightly bombing. Hitler later abandoned his invasion plans, but torpedoed supply ships, attempting to starve the island nation into surrender. The newspaperman Edward R. Murrow rallied American opinion behind the beleaguered British with his live radio reports from London.

At this juncture, FDR did everything in his power to help the British government. He lent it fifty or sixty destroyers, even though the United States (at the time) was maintaining its position of neutrality.

However, he had to contend with powerful isolationist currents in the United States, particularly among Midwest Republicans such as the publisher of the *Chicago Tribune*, Col. Robert McCormick.

America First

The America First Committee actively opposed U.S. intervention in World War II. Begun in 1940, it included a number of prominent industrialists as well as probably the most famous man of his day: the aviator Charles Lindbergh. The committee dissolved after the Japanese attack on Pearl Harbor in 1941.

THE UNITED STATES ENTERS THE WAR

From Pearl Harbor to V-E Day

Japan had sought to become a dominant force in Asia in order to increase its influence and acquire the raw materials it lacked. The island nation believed that it had to expand and seize other parts of Asia such as China and the Pacific Islands. Nationalism had grown in Japan during the 1930s just as it had in Germany. Loyalty toward Emperor Hirohito was drilled into young children, who revered the man not only as a leader, but as a god. When Japan attacked China, it found itself fighting not one but two forces—the Chinese Nationalists, led by Chiang Kai-shek, as well as the Chinese Communists with their leader Mao Zedong. America preferred the Nationalists, yet was determined to remain neutral.

Relations between the United States and the Japanese had deteriorated prior to the Pearl Harbor attack. The United States, along with much of the rest of the world, had condemned the expansion of Japanese power in Asia and the South Pacific. Government officials believed a Japanese attack was imminent, but strongly suspected that it would occur in the South Pacific Islands (such as the Philippines). As the Japanese attacked Pearl Harbor on Oahu on that peaceful Sunday, the new radar technology had detected blips on the screen, but most believed they were U.S. aircraft.

The attack crippled nearly all of the U.S. battleships; the *Arizona* exploded into a blaze five stories high. Four-fifths of her crew died instantly. The only vessels to escape the onslaught were two aircraft carriers, which had been at sea—the *Lexington* and the *Enterprise*.

These two ships would soon have surprises of their own for the Japanese.

Remembering the Dead

The USS *Arizona* Memorial was established to honor the servicemen who perished during the surprise attack on December 7, 1941. More than 1,000 sailors went down with the sunken ship and remain buried at sea. The hull lies about forty feet beneath the memorial and can be seen from above.

FDR RESPONDS

In 1940, FDR made history. Never before had a president served longer than two terms, or eight years. President Roosevelt's leadership was pulling the nation out of its economic depths, and the public rewarded him with a third term. Seeing Europe embroiled in conflict, Roosevelt tried his best to remain neutral, though he viewed the world stage cautiously.

No one could deny the prudence of appropriating funds for American warships and airplanes. Congress passed the first peacetime draft. Still, isolationists believed that the oceans on either side of the American continent would protect it from war. That sentiment changed dramatically after the Pearl Harbor attacks, which killed more than 2,300 servicemen and nearly 100 civilians. President Roosevelt, reflecting the mood of an outraged nation, called on Congress the next day with these remarks:

> Yesterday, December 7, 1941—a date which will live in infamy—the United States of America was suddenly and deliberately attacked by naval and air forces of the Empire of Japan.

The United States was at peace with that nation and, at the solicitation of Japan, was still in conversation with the Government and its Emperor looking toward the maintenance of peace in the Pacific .... As Commander-in-Chief of the Army and Navy, I have directed that all measures be taken for our defense. ... With confidence in our armed forces—with the unbounding determination of our people—we will gain the inevitable triumph—so help us God.

I ask that the Congress declare that since the unprovoked and dastardly attack by Japan on Sunday, December Seventh, a state of war has existed between the United States and the Japanese empire.

Three days after the Hawaiian attack, Germany and Italy declared war on the United States. Americans found themselves immersed in the war effort, with emotions running high. During the early months of 1942, more than 100,000 Japanese Americans (though they were U.S. citizens) were relocated into internment camps. Anti-Japanese sentiment crossed to hysteria as these citizens were forced to leave their homes and jobs to live under the harsh conditions of the camps. It's reported that President Roosevelt opposed this relocation measure, but that he bowed to public pressure. After he was re-elected in 1944, Roosevelt ordered the camps closed.

MAJOR WWII BATTLES IN THE SOUTH PACIFIC

After the bombing of Pearl Harbor, the United States engaged the Empire of Japan in battles across the South Pacific. In particular, the Battle of the Coral Sea (fought in early May 1942) was a turning point that effectively checked the Japanese advance to the south. Admiral Chester Nimitz, privy to decoded enemy messages of the Japanese, tried to thwart their plans to cut off Australia. The USS *Lexington* was sunk and the USS *Yorktown* damaged. The Japanese retired from this battle with heavy losses.

BATTLE OF MIDWAY

Attempting to destroy the remaining U.S. Pacific fleet at this important naval outpost, the Japanese hadn't counted on American naval reconnaissance planes observing their armada from a distance. In June 1942, U.S. carriers ambushed Japanese carriers descending on the Midway Islands. Four Japanese carriers were sunk. The U.S. victory at Midway dashed any Japanese hopes to invade Hawaii. Coming on the heels of the Battle of the Coral Sea, it gave the United States supremacy at sea in the South Pacific.

Chief U.S. Commanders in World War II

- Gen. Dwight D. Eisenhower, Supreme Allied Commander
- Gen. George Marshall, U.S. Army Chief of Staff
- Gen. Douglas McArthur
- Gen. Omar Bradley
- Gen. Mark Clark
- Gen. George S. Patton
- Adm. Chester Nimitz

IWO JIMA

Though a tiny volcanic island merely five miles long, its airstrips were vital for American short-range aircraft targeting Japan. Air strikes preceded the U.S. Marines' landing on February 19, 1945. The brutal struggle was unlike anything Europe had seen. More than 6,000 U.S. Marines lost their lives capturing the island from the Japanese (whose losses were estimated at 20,000). The campaign concluded on March 16 of that year.

WAR IN AFRICA AND EUROPE

U.S. troops took part in the invasion of North Africa in 1943 and slowly fought their way up the Italian peninsula. In the wake of Hitler's invasion of the Soviet Union in June 1941, the Soviets had joined the Allied camp, and Stalin urged the Allies to open a second front in Europe to take pressure off the hard-pressed Soviet troops in the East.

It became clear that a French invasion to liberate Europe was pivotal to any plan for defeating Hitler. But the Germans felt certain that the Allies would cross the English Channel at its narrowest point (Calais). Eisenhower and the Allies played on this misconception, deceiving the Germans with a fake buildup precisely at Calais.

Dubbed Operation Overlord (a name coined by Winston Churchill), the invasion of France would take place in Normandy on what the Allies termed "D-Day." Amphibious forces from the United States, Canada, and Britain would storm five beaches code-named Utah, Omaha (both stormed by American troops), Juno (stormed by Canadian troops), Sword, and Gold (both stormed by British troops).

Three airborne divisions would also be dropped to protect the invading troops.

Clicking Like Crickets

When soldiers dropped from parachutes during the D-Day invasion, they were so scattered about on land that in order to identify one another as Allied forces they used clicker devices that made the sound of a cricket. This way, they could remain fairly quiet before facing enemy forces.

The mission called for just the right weather conditions to be successful. Severe wind and rain postponed the crossing by one day. General Eisenhower okayed the invasion to begin on June 6 when the weather cooperated. Though he dreaded a disaster, Eisenhower knew he had to move forward with the plan. In case the invasion collapsed, Eisenhower had drafted a speech that he carried with him stating, "Our landings . . . have failed. . . . The troops, the Air and Navy did all that bravery and devotion to duty could do. If any blame or fault attaches to the attempt, it is mine alone."

Though this was not to be the anticipated landing site, the Germans had still booby-trapped the French landscape, making it difficult to land gliders or bring boats ashore. The worst fighting came at Omaha, as the Americans had landed in the midst of a German defense area. The tide had risen and fallen, the terrain was difficult, and many of the landing maps were inaccurate. At least 5,000 men perished, but soon Omaha Beach and the surrounding areas were secured. Not long after, forces forged out into the Normandy countryside and began making their way toward Paris.

As the Normandy beaches were secured, it was no longer necessary to use artificial harbors (called "Mulberries") because Cherbourg was a genuine port, allowing replacements and supplies ashore. Fighting at Caen left that ancient town a pile of rubble, but on August 25, the Allies marched triumphantly through the streets of Paris.

BATTLE OF THE BULGE

After the Normandy invasion, Allied forces swept through France but stalled along the German border that September. From intelligence reports, the Allies realized that the Germans were within striking distance of Antwerp. A particularly harsh winter also hindered defense efforts. In December 1944, General George Patton pushed his troops through Bastogne, Belgium, in forty-eight hours, a feat others swore he couldn't manage. Germany's Panzer Division proved as stubborn as the U.S. general. Their aim was to lay siege to Antwerp, but their advance was halted near the Meuse River. The Allied success took weeks to accomplish, with the help of air power pushing the Germans back to their own lines in January.

As the Allies closed in on the German frontier, Hitler surprised them with an attack through the Ardennes Forest, a campaign later called the Battle of the Bulge. Hitler reasoned that if the Germans cut off Allied supplies at Antwerp, Belgium, it would prevent their moving into his homeland. German troops fooled the weary Allies by dressing in G.I. uniforms. Poor weather had rendered Allied aircraft useless.

The Germans had hoped to stop the Allies as they crossed the Rhine, but American forces used the Ludendorff Bridge, which the Germans had failed to destroy. The Red Army pushed toward Berlin as Germans scuttled to protect their women, children, and property. The Soviets reached Berlin on April 22, but with Hitler's orders that even children mount a defense, it took another ten days for the city to surrender. Hitler's SS squads (the secret state police) publicly executed anyone refusing to obey and fight.

Battle of Stalingrad

In late 1942 through early 1943, this battle proved a turning point in the European war. Stalingrad was a strategically located industrial center and a vital German target. After heavy fighting, the Germans could no longer sustain their losses, and the Soviets were able to prevail. There ended the German advance into the USSR, though much of Stalingrad was destroyed. Thus, the Soviets forced the Germans west while the other Allied armies drove the Germans east, pushing them back to the Rhine.

HITLER'S DEMISE

On April 30, 1945, Hitler and his new wife, Eva Braun, realizing that Berlin was finally falling, committed suicide in the bunker in which they had lived for the past six months. The Nazis burned their bodies. Hitler's Third Reich was literally reduced to ashes.

After the Americans and Soviets converged in Germany in April 1945, Berlin fell to the Allies at the month's end. As his last significant act before his suicide, Hitler named Grand Admiral Karl Doenitz to succeed him as chief of state. General Alfred Jodl, Doenitz's representative, signed the surrender document at Eisenhower's headquarters in Reims on May 7. Forces elsewhere in Europe had already thrown down their arms. The full and unconditional surrender took effect at one minute past midnight after a second signing in Berlin with Soviet participation. May 8, 1945, would forever after be known as V-E Day, short for Victory in Europe.

LIFE ON THE HOME FRONT

Pulling Together for the Boys

Once President Roosevelt asked for a declaration of war, the country rallied together to support the war effort. The increased industrialization stimulated the sluggish economy, which was climbing out of the Great Depression. As military production rose, and with men conscripted into the armed services, women took jobs or volunteered in staffing weapon factories. This quickly earned females the nickname "Rosie the Riveter."

With so many raw materials needed for the war, rationing became a way of life. The emergency Office of Price Administration (OPA) was created to oversee the rationing goods. Rationing was undertaken in conjunction with price and rent controls as well.

RATIONING FORCES CREATIVE MEASURES

Women, accustomed to wearing nylon or silk stockings, had to do without these. Some drew a black line down the back of their legs with an eyebrow pencil to give the appearance of a seamed stocking. Of course, where there is limited supply and great demand, the illegal or black market flourishes. Ration coupons, stamps, and certificates were used for items in short supply.

Rationed items included:

- Tires
- Cars
- Gasoline
- Shoes
- Sugar
- Coffee
- Meat
- Cheese
- Bicycles

In addition, many families planted victory gardens in their backyards to supplement their diets, allowing commercial farms to supply food for the troops. The war provided the impetus some farmers needed to experiment with crop rotation and better fertilizers. Everyone, it seemed, became frugal, industrious, and resourceful, not because they wanted to, but because they had to.

Was There Really a Private Ryan?

In the movie *Saving Private Ryan,* a detail of soldiers are sent to remove the only remaining Ryan son from combat duty. Did this sort of thing really happen?

The Sole Survivor Policy is a set of regulations that protects members of a family from the draft or combat duty if they have already lost family members in military service. The regulations were a response to the loss of the five Sullivan brothers who were all killed when the USS *Juneau* was sunk during World War II.

Mail and packages between loved ones in the States and the troops overseas were government inspected. At times, portions of letters were cut out for fear critical information would fall into enemy hands. Citizens back home also purchased war bonds to help finance the effort. For many of the young recruits, their experience in World War II would serve as the defining moment of their lives.

In 1944, Congress passed the Servicemen's Readjustment Act, better known as the "G.I. Bill." This was a benefits package for returning veterans that spawned a postwar baby and housing boom. It established veterans' hospitals around the country where vets could obtain rehabilitation and medical care and provided low-interest mortgages, college tuition, and trade-school funds.

ROOSEVELT'S DEATH

Roosevelt, Churchill, and Stalin met at the Soviet Black Sea port of Yalta in February 1945 to formulate Allied military strategy and declare an end to German militarism and Nazism. In addition, they expressed determination that war criminals would be brought to swift and just punishment.

The United Nations

Leaders at the Yalta Conference called for a conference of nations to promote world peace and cooperation following the war. On April 25, 1945, delegates from fifty nations met in San Francisco to draft a charter. The charter was ratified by the U.S. Senate on July 28, 1945. The United Nations (UN), with its home in New York City, was adopted on October 24, 1945, to foster better relations and encourage respect for human rights. Member nations pledged to settle differences peacefully.

Franklin Delano Roosevelt died of natural causes at his home in Warm Springs, Georgia, in April 1945. The only president to be elected four times was mourned by the entire country, if not the world. Sadly, the man whose administration was plagued by the actions of Hitler and the Japanese died before any surrender or victory. Vice

President Harry S. Truman was sworn in as the nation's thirty-third president on April 12, 1945.

BUILDING THE BOMB

In 1932, British scientist James Chadwick discovered an atomic particle, the neutron, which could penetrate the nucleus of an atom and cause it to separate. The divided atom would release more neutrons, causing other atoms to split. As the chain reaction progressed and built up, an enormous amount of energy would be released.

During the first days of World War II, leading physicists such as Albert Einstein suspected that Germany was already at work to create a massive weapon of annihilation, better known as the atomic or A-bomb. They pooled their knowledge, and in 1939 Einstein wrote the president to tell him of their suspicions. Fortunately, the president heeded the warning.

Einstein's Letter to Roosevelt

Albert Einstein, best known for his theory of relativity, collaborated with several physicists in writing to President Roosevelt to warn him of possible German attempts to make the atomic bomb. This lent urgency to American efforts to build the A-bomb, but Einstein played no role in the work and had no knowledge of what would be called the Manhattan Project.

In 1942, many prominent scientists began developing the A-bomb in the small New Mexico community of Los Alamos (as well as at sites in Oak Ridge, Tennessee, and Hanaford, Washington). The undertaking was termed "the Manhattan Project" because some of the work took place at Columbia University. Physicists Enrico Fermi and J. Robert Oppenheimer worked on the Manhattan Project, as did many other prominent scientists, including some who had fled fascism in Europe. U.S. Army engineer General Leslie Groves headed the project that at one time involved approximately 600,000 people.

THE BOMB PUT TO USE

After V-E Day, the war in the Pacific theater still raged on. American bombing raids on Japan's industrial centers met with limited success. Radar, still in its infancy, proved too unreliable to use in designating targets. Even B-29 bombing raids aimed at residential and civilian targets didn't convince the Japanese to surrender, and the raids were proving to be costly as well.

Destroyer of Worlds

Oppenheimer later wrote that when he saw the flash in the desert and the mushroom cloud rising into the air, what came into his mind was a quotation from the Indian epic *The Bhagavad-Gita*: "I am become Death, destroyer of worlds." After the war, Oppenheimer's opposition to developing the H-bomb led the government, in the grip of anticommunist hysteria, to revoke his security clearance.

With the Manhattan Project, U.S. scientists proved they could use the explosive power of nuclear fission rather than TNT to wreak mass destruction. Oppenheimer and his team tested the A-bomb near Alamogordo, New Mexico, on July 16, 1945. No one knew whether it would work until a tremendous blast rushed across the desert. Oppenheimer's team informed President Truman that it had indeed worked.

Although the bomb had originally been created for possible use against Hitler's Third Reich, Truman now faced a crucial decision—whether to use the A-bomb against the Japanese in order to end the war. Truman didn't want to risk the lives of American servicemen in a potential invasion of Japan, and it's said he had little to no hesitation in using this powerful new weapon. At Potsdam (outside Berlin in July 1945), Churchill agreed that Truman should use the A-bomb.

At 8:15 A.M. on August 6, 1945, an American B-29 bomber named the *Enola Gay* ferried the bomb to Hiroshima, the Japanese city chosen for the drop. There, it exploded about 2,000 feet above the ground, producing a fireball hotter than the surface of the sun and leveling several square miles. Atomic radiation and searing heat vaporized everything in its range.

Surprisingly, Japan didn't ask for terms of surrender following the attack on Hiroshima. So on August 9, another B-29 bomber dropped an A-bomb on the city of Nagasaki, causing almost as much destruction as the first bombing. (Some historians have speculated that the United States dropped the second bomb as a means of demonstrating to the Soviet Union that America had a nuclear arsenal and not merely a single bomb.)

Death by Radiation

While the bomb itself immediately killed approximately 45,000 people in Hiroshima, its effects, as well as that of the bomb dropped on Nagasaki, continued to be felt long afterward. It's estimated that the Hiroshima bomb killed 90,000–166,000 people altogether, while the Nagasaki bomb killed 60,000–80,000.

Meanwhile, the Soviet Union had declared war on Japan on August 8, destroying its army in China and taking over most of occupied Manchuria. The Red Army was continuing its move into Korea as Japan finally surrendered to the Allies on August 15, 1945. This wasn't an unconditional surrender, as the Allies agreed that the Japanese could keep their emperor. The formal signing took place on September 2 in Tokyo Bay aboard the battleship *Missouri* with an American delegation headed by General MacArthur, who then became the military governor of Allied-occupied Japan.

MCCARTHYISM

1950s Witch-Hunt

In a speech given in Fulton, Missouri, on March 5, 1946, Winston Churchill declared:

> From Stettin in the Baltic to Trieste in the Adriatic an "Iron Curtain" has descended across the continent. Behind that line lie all the capitals of the ancient states of Central and Eastern Europe. Warsaw, Berlin, Prague, Vienna, Budapest, Belgrade, Bucharest and Sofia; all these famous cities and the populations around them lie in what I must call the Soviet sphere, and all are subject . . . not only to Soviet influence but to a very high and in some cases increasing measure of control from Moscow.

The speech marked the formal beginning of what came to be called the Cold War, a decades-long tension between the United States and other Western powers on the one hand and the Soviet Union and its allies on the other. In America, the first decade of the Cold War was marked by increasing levels of paranoia about Communist infiltration and subversion.

During the 1940s, President Truman ordered the investigation of applicants for government jobs for Communist connections. Various government agencies were formed to provide intelligence about Communist activities. The FBI, under its monomaniacal leader J. Edgar Hoover, was given a blank check to combat anything it viewed as "Communist-inspired."

Yet Truman faced criticism that he hadn't gone far enough. In 1948, American writer and editor Whittaker Chambers testified before Representative Richard Nixon and the House Committee on Un-American Activities that he'd been a member of the Communist Party in the 1920s and 1930s, and that he'd transmitted secret information to Soviet agents. He charged that Alger Hiss, a member of the State Department, was a Communist and that Hiss turned over classified documents to him. Although Hiss denied the charges, Chambers produced document copies implicating Hiss in the matter. After a probe by the Department of Justice, Hiss was indicted for perjury. His first jury failed to reach a verdict, but his second trial in January 1950 handed him a conviction.

THE SPREAD OF COMMUNISM

American concern with Communism seemed well founded to many people. In China the Nationalist government of Chiang Kai-shek (which the United States had supported) could not withstand the onslaught of Communist forces led by Mao Zedong. By the end of 1949, government troops had been defeated, forcing Chiang into exile on Taiwan. Elated by victory, Mao formed the People's Republic of China. Truman's critics charged that the administration failed to support the anti-Communist movement in China to its fullest ability. It didn't make anyone less nervous when Truman also announced that the Soviet Union had developed its own atomic bomb. Soon, fallout shelters were built and stocked with provisions in the event of atomic attack.

In 1952, in the Marshall Islands, the United States conducted tests on a weapon of even greater magnitude. In fact, the hydrogen bomb, or H-bomb, was 500 times more powerful than the atomic bomb dropped on Hiroshima. This thermonuclear device was powered by a fusion reaction rather than the fission reaction of the A-bomb.

Nuclear Bomb Drills

Millions of American schoolchildren took part in atomic bomb drills, which lasted well into the 1960s. During these drills, the children ducked beneath their desks, an action intended to keep them safe from flying glass. Of course, nothing could keep them safe from the actual bomb or its accompanying radiation, but teachers weren't encouraged to explain that to their students.

THINGS START TO GET OUT OF HAND

Many opposed the H-bomb's development, including well-known scientists, but it was thought that the Soviets would produce their own. Although it was terrifying, this new superbomb equipped the United States with a powerful deterrent—or, heaven forbid, weapon—in any future conflict.

In 1957, the Soviet Union successfully launched the first man-made object placed in orbit, called *Sputnik*. This event also fueled fears that the USSR was gaining important ground in the sciences, overtaking the United States. Congress passed the National Defense Education Act the following year to enable scholarships and laboratories for science students, who had to sign an oath vowing they had no Communist sympathies.

"I HAVE IN MY HAND A LIST"

Communist fear festered within government ranks. In February 1950, Senator Joseph R. McCarthy of Wisconsin charged that the State Department knowingly employed more than 200 Communists. In a speech given in 1950 to the Republican Women's Club of Wheeling, West Virginia, McCarthy declared:

> I have here in my hand a list of 205 [State Department employees] that were known to the Secretary of State as being members of the Communist Party and who nevertheless are still working and shaping policy in the State Department.

He later revised his claim to a much lower number, and after an investigation, all of his charges were proved to be false. But McCarthy, as chairman of the Permanent Subcommittee on Investigations of the Senate Operations Committee, continued to accuse others of Communist sympathies, often without any evidence. He launched investigations of the Voice of America as well as the U.S. Army Signal Corps. J. Edgar Hoover and the FBI assisted McCarthy in hunting Communist spies and sympathizers.

The McCarran Act

Congress passed the McCarran Internal Security Act in 1950, forcing the registration of all Communist organizations and allowing the government to intern Communists during national emergencies. It also prohibited those people from doing any defense work and prohibited entry into the United States to members of "totalitarian" organizations or governments. The act was passed over President Truman's veto.

Such behavior became known as McCarthyism, meaning any unfounded accusation of subversive activities. Not only were government officials accused and interrogated, but also film directors, military officers, and others from all walks of life were brought before Senate hearings to name those they knew with Communist ties. As a result, many reputations were ruined and careers left in shambles. A few of the accused even committed suicide.

The Hollywood Ten

The House Un-American Activities Committee (HUAC) became particularly notorious for calling witnesses before it whom it accused of subversion and demanding that as the price for clearing their names, they name others—whom the committee could then call. HUAC's investigations of the entertainment industry received particularly wide publicity.

A group of ten Hollywood writers and directors, however, refused to answer the committee's questions (they were Alvah Bessie, Herbert Biberman, Lester Cole, Edward Dmytryk, Ring Lardner Jr., John Howard Lawson, Albert Maltz, Samuel Ornitz, Adrian Scott, and Dalton Trumbo). They were held in contempt of Congress and sentenced to prison terms.

Senator Margaret Chase Smith, lambasting her Senate colleagues, said, "Freedom of speech is not what it used to be in America." President Truman warned of the fear and hysteria wrought by Senator McCarthy, for the senator even accused the U.S. Army of Communist infiltration. By 1954, his Senate colleagues censured McCarthy for abusing his powers. A known alcoholic, Joseph McCarthy died of liver damage a few years later.

THE KOREAN WAR

The Cold War Gets Hot

As World War II was raging, the Allied powers had agreed that once Japan was defeated, Korea would become an independent state. After Japan's surrender, General Douglas MacArthur's plan called for the creation of an artificial line at the 38th parallel in Korea. The line essentially split the country in half. The Japanese forces above the parallel surrendered to the Soviet Union, and those to the south to the Americans.

In June 1950, the Communist government of North Korea launched a full-scale military invasion of neighboring South Korea, a capitalist country.

The United Nations Security Council voted 9–0 to hold North Korea accountable for the attack. The resolution sent a peacekeeping force, virtually all of which was made up of U.S. troops. The Soviet Union was a permanent member of the Security Council, but it had been boycotting meetings because other members refused to recognize the Communist government in China as the rightful government of the Chinese people.

THE KOREAN "POLICE ACTION"

Not wanting to call these actions involvement in a war, President Truman termed the conflict a police action and put General MacArthur in command of the UN forces, a post he would hold until his replacement in April 1951. MacArthur held his position on the southeastern portion of the peninsula, and American bombing missions crippled North Korean supply lines.

In one of his boldest military operations, General MacArthur planned for a large amphibious landing on the west coast of South Korea at Inchon. Once ashore, American troops would push back the enemy and recapture the capital of Seoul. Concurrently, the Eighth Army would break out of the Pusan Perimeter and head toward Seoul as well. Despite skepticism, MacArthur pushed for his plan. American forces hit the beaches in September, taking the capital on September 27, 1950. Many thought the war was over with the UN goals having been achieved. The Communists were contained behind the 38th parallel.

SOUTH KOREA PUSHES NORTH

The Americans had done so well, however, that the South Koreans and MacArthur believed they could push farther to expel Communism from Korea completely. Others in Washington didn't concur, knowing how strongly China and the Soviet Union felt that North Korea served as a buffer state. Syngman Rhee, president of South Korea, was determined to fight regardless of American sentiment. His troops crossed the 38th parallel and attacked the North Koreans. When they did, President Truman immediately committed UN forces (with the majority of them being U.S. soldiers) to follow Rhee. The next month, Truman and MacArthur met on Wake Island, hoping to discuss the final phase of the Korean War, which they anticipated ending by Thanksgiving.

Arrogant in both his confidence and his assumptions about his political as well as military responsibilities, MacArthur violated Truman's instructions and advanced his men too close to the Chinese border. MacArthur had seriously underestimated the Chinese forces, leaving the Americans vulnerable. By November, it was evident that China was invading on a much larger scale.

MacArthur outwardly opposed some of the restraints on his command, but Washington officials feared that the Soviet Union would view the Korean conflict as a global struggle, sparking another world war. President Truman's concern over this as well as his desire to show that the American military was firmly under civilian control eventually led to his replacing MacArthur with General Matthew Ridgway. General MacArthur faced a Senate hearing for his insubordination to the commander in chief—threatening the Chinese with a powerful U.S.-UN attack without clearing it first with Truman.

FIGHTING ENDS

Back home, General Dwight D. Eisenhower and his running mate Richard Nixon won the presidential election in 1952. Though peace negotiations had begun in 1951, the new administration inherited the war, and fighting continued for two more years until an armistice was signed on July 27, 1953. In the final analysis, the war cost everyone in lives and materials and left no country satisfied—certainly not the United States.

After Joseph Stalin died in 1953, Nikita Khrushchev exposed the brutal crimes that Stalin had committed against his own people. He'd ruled with terror, executing millions of Soviet citizens. These revelations softened the tensions with the West, but only slightly. The United States committed more funds to NATO (the North Atlantic Treaty Organization), and it stepped up aid to another government it believed was in danger of Communist takeover—the small southeast Asian country of Vietnam.

MARTIN LUTHER KING JR. AND CIVIL RIGHTS

Fighting Jim Crow

Throughout the southern United States, and in many parts of the north, African Americans remained second-class citizens. They were subject to constant humiliation and discrimination, as well as in some cases horrific violence. A series of laws in the South made discrimination explicit: African Americans were forbidden to drink from the same water fountains as whites, to use the same entrances, to swim in the same pools. They were prevented from voting by outlandish requirements and "tests" that were skewed against them. These laws, collectively, became known as "Jim Crow" laws.

Beginning in the late 1950s, a new generation of black activists began organizing protests against Jim Crow. The most important of these occurred in Montgomery, Alabama.

THE BUS BOYCOTT

African Americans riding buses were required, as a matter of course, to give up their seats to whites and to sit at the back of the bus. On December 1, 1955, an African-American seamstress named Rosa Parks, on her way home in Montgomery, refused to give up her seat. She was arrested and subsequently tried, found guilty, and fined.

The local head of the National Association for the Advancement of Colored People (NAACP), E.D. Nixon, met with various local ministers. One of these was a young man named Martin Luther King Jr., who had studied the philosophy and tactics of nonviolence and was particularly influenced by the example of Mahatma Gandhi and the struggle for Indian independence from Great Britain. King believed such tactics could be used to oppose Jim Crow laws.

King and his supporters organized a boycott of buses in Montgomery. Blacks walked to work, car-pooled, or found other means of transportation. The boycott rapidly grew in effectiveness.

White Racists Strike Back

The city's power structure and groups such as the White Citizens' Council countered the boycott by ordering police to arrest blacks walking to work for "loitering" or "jaywalking"—even if they were on the sidewalk. African-American cabdrivers who kept their fares low for boycotters were fined. In an escalation of the violence, King's house was firebombed.

King's answer to violence was:

"We must love our white brothers, no matter what they do to us. We must make them know that we love them. Jesus still cries out in words that echo across the centuries: 'Love your enemies; bless them that curse you; pray for them that despitefully use you.' This is what we must live by."

The boycott was successful. But it was just the beginning.

In the early 1960s James Meredith made headlines when he tried to enroll in the all-white University of Mississippi and the governor personally blocked his attempts despite federal law. President John

F. Kennedy had sent in federal marshals. Governor George Wallace of Alabama blocked the University of Alabama, swearing to prevent integration, and once again, Kennedy sent in the National Guard. Such incidents incited the president to propose a bill on desegregation, and his successor would push through significant civil rights legislation.

King, along with other black leaders, organized an August 1963 March on Washington for civil rights. More than 300,000 crowded around the Lincoln Memorial and the Reflecting Pool to listen to speakers. When King stepped to the podium, he made his remarks, and then one of his aides yelled, "Tell them about the dream, Martin." Inspired, King said:

"Now is the time to make real the promises of democracy. Now is the time to rise from the dark and desolate valley of segregation to the sunlit path of racial justice. Now is the time to open the doors of opportunity to all of God's children. . . . I have a dream that one day this nation will rise up and live out the true meaning of its creed: 'We hold these truths to be self-evident; that all men are created equal.' I have a dream that one day on the red hills of Georgia the sons of former slaves and the sons of former slave owners will be able to sit down together at the table of brotherhood. . . . I have a dream that my four little children will one day live in a nation where they will not be judged by the color of their skin but by the content of their character. I have a dream today. . . .

"When we let freedom ring, when we let it ring from every village and every hamlet, from every state and every city, we will be able to speed up that day when all of God's children, black men and white men, Jews and Gentiles, Protestants and Catholics, will be able to join hands and sing in the words of the old Negro spiritual, 'Free at last! Free at last! Thank God Almighty, we are free at last!'"

King's speech showed not only his articulate and passionate delivery, but also his moral character, and it gave momentum to his followers and their cause. As a result of his work, he was awarded the Nobel Peace Prize in 1964.

A HERO FALLS

Continuing his work to speak out for equality, King made another speech in Memphis, Tennessee, on April 3, 1968, where he said, "We've got some difficult days ahead, but it really doesn't matter to me now, because I've been to the mountaintop." The next evening, on April 4, an assassin gunned down Martin Luther King Jr. as he stood on the balcony of his Memphis motel.

BLACK POWER

Angry Voices

While millions were thrilled by Martin Luther King Jr.'s words, many young African Americans were impatient with what they saw as the glacial pace of change in the United States. Others had no confidence in the government's promises of improvement.

Among the most dynamic and influential of these was Malcolm Little, better known as Malcolm X. As a leader of the Nation of Islam, he attracted a large following. In the last year of his life, after breaking from the Nation, he began moving in a different, and in some ways more radical direction.

MALCOLM X

Malcolm was born in 1925 to parents active in the Garvey movement, which supported a return to Africa by blacks. He grew to manhood involved in a life of petty crime and street hustling. He was arrested for burglary in 1946 and sent to prison. There he met members of the Nation of Islam, a black separatist sect led by Elijah Muhammad. Malcolm was fascinated by their teachings and quickly joined.

In the Nation, Malcolm's oratorical gifts pushed him to the forefront, and he rose to be Elijah Muhammad's chief assistant. In his speeches, he preached that whites are inherently evil and that no cooperation or equal interaction could occur between the two races. However, as time went on, Malcolm began gradually to question these assertions. He saw the power of the civil rights movement and was disturbed by Elijah Muhammad's decision to remain aloof from it. He also was horrified to learn that the leader of the Nation had regularly conducted sexual affairs with a variety of young women.

The Garvey Movement

Marcus Garvey, despairing of ever getting just treatment from whites in America, formed the Universal Negro Improvement Association for the purpose of setting up African-American institutions and eventually facilitating a return to Africa by American blacks. Although influential (at its peak, the UNIA had 4 million members), the organization was divided by quarrels and eventually collapsed.

In March 1964 Malcolm publicly broke with the Nation and declared his allegiance to mainstream Islam. Further, he declared, it was possible—even desirable—to work with white activists toward common goals. He founded the Organization of Afro-American Unity and met, albeit briefly, with Martin Luther King Jr. He began to suggest in his speeches that the problems of black people in the United States were more fundamental than just racism, that there was a systemic problem that must be addressed.

In February 1965, while addressing a meeting in Harlem, Malcolm X was gunned down by several men in the crowd. Suspicion turned immediately upon the Nation of Islam, and although the assassins were identified as members of the Nation, there has never been definitive proof that the organization's leadership ordered the assassination.

INSPIRED BY MALCOLM X

Many younger black leaders of the civil rights movement looked to Malcolm for inspiration as well as to King. Among them were:

- Stokely Carmichael, leader of the Student Non-Violent Coordinating Committee (SNCC)
- Angela Davis, radical professor and activist
- Huey Newton and Bobby Seale, founders of the Black Panther Party

JOHN F. KENNEDY

The New Frontier

As Americans approached the 1960 presidential election, life was good. Americans reveled in their music and the stardom of movie icons such as Marilyn Monroe and Marlon Brando, and they enjoyed the new medium of television.

Many assumed that since Eisenhower had been a popular president, Vice President Richard Nixon would easily win the 1960 election as the Republican nominee. To beat Nixon, Democrats selected a dashing senator from Massachusetts who was certainly groomed if not destined for the presidency. John F. Kennedy (known by his famous initials JFK) had a successful and wealthy father (Joseph P. Kennedy, who had served in the New Deal administration of Franklin Roosevelt) and maternal grandfather (John F. Fitzgerald, also known as Honey Fitz, who had been the mayor of Boston many years before).

Movie Producer

One of Joseph Kennedy's activities was movie producer. In the 1920s, he formed R.K.O., a film studio responsible for hundreds of successful movies. He also conducted an extensive affair with movie star Gloria Swanson, backing the never-completed vehicle for her, *Queen Kelly.*

Although Kennedy had the intellect, connections, charm, and World War II heroism (the rescue of his PT-109 crew off the Solomon Islands was well known), he faced certain challenge as the first Irish

Catholic to seek executive office. Choosing a Southern running mate—Lyndon B. Johnson of Texas—balanced the Democratic ticket.

During Kennedy's acceptance speech at the Democratic convention, he said:

> "We stand at the edge of a New Frontier—the frontier of unfulfilled hopes and dreams. It will deal with unsolved problems of peace and war, unconquered pockets of ignorance and prejudice, unanswered questions of poverty and surplus."

The term New Frontier was then used for his domestic and foreign policies.

In a series of debates, the first ever to be televised, the candidates squared off. Their race remained close, but most agreed that Kennedy seemed much more poised on camera, which emphasized Nixon's haggard appearance. That finesse paid off at the polls, where Kennedy edged ahead in a very narrow defeat of Richard Nixon. In fact, Kennedy garnered 49.7 percent of the popular vote to Nixon's 49.6, though he clearly won the electoral votes needed (303 to Nixon's 219).

At forty-three, Kennedy was the youngest president ever elected (Theodore Roosevelt was slightly younger when he became president, but he had not been elected). In his dynamic inaugural address, Kennedy challenged his fellow Americans with "Ask not what your country can do for you—ask what you can do for your country." He energized the nation with his idea of a new frontier, and subsequently inspired a generation to public service, particularly with the Peace Corps, which rallied professional and skilled Americans to work in developing nations.

These initiatives served Kennedy's clear vision of volunteerism, freedom, and equality for all—as well as technological achievement, as he pledged that the United States would land a man on the moon by the end of the decade. With his stylish wife Jacqueline and the couple's young children, Kennedy rose to near-royal status in the public's eye.

THE MISSILES OF OCTOBER

One Minute to Midnight

In January 1959, following a revolution on the Caribbean island of Cuba, President Fulgencio Batista fled to the Dominican Republic. For much of the 1950s he had run a police state that favored the wealthy. Fidel Castro led the Cuban rebels—known as "the bearded ones"—along with his second-in-command, Ernesto "Che" Guevara. Triumphant, they took Havana, the capital, making Castro the Cuban leader.

The United States broke diplomatic relations with Cuba in early 1961, and Castro turned to the Soviet Union for assistance. This brought the threat of Communism within ninety miles of U.S. shores, and it was an unsettling factor for both the outgoing Eisenhower and incoming Kennedy administrations.

On April 19, 1961, approximately 1,500 Cuban exiles returned to the island to mount an invasion they hoped would incite an uprising and topple the Castro regime. Although no U.S. forces were deployed, U.S. support of what became known as the Bay of Pigs incident was undeniable. The CIA had trained antirevolutionary exiles under the Eisenhower administration, and Kennedy approved the invasion. Armed with U.S. weapons, the exiles landed at the Bahía de Cochinos (Bay of Pigs) on Cuba's southern coast. Castro's army quickly discovered them, killing about ninety and taking the rest as prisoners. The invasion was not only a failure, but also an embarrassment for the Kennedy administration, which was blamed for not fully supporting it and for allowing it to occur in the first place. Although the captured Cuban exiles were later let off with ransom, the entire incident set the world stage for increased tensions between the superpowers: the United States and the Soviet Union.

Bay of Pigs and Watergate

The Bay of Pigs returned to haunt the American presidency more than a decade later when it turned out that at least one of the Watergate burglars, Bernard Barker, had taken part in the planning of the attempted invasion. (Ironically, another of the burglars, Frank Sturgis, had fought with Castro forces during the revolution and then later trained a group of anti-Castro exiles.)

This unease culminated the next year when U.S. reconnaissance missions flying over Cuba photographed Soviet-managed construction work and spotted a ballistic missile in October 1962. Castro, certain that the United States would try another invasion, had agreed to Soviet missiles for his island's protection.

Without alarming the nation, President Kennedy consulted his top advisors to discuss options—an invasion, air strikes, a blockade, or diplomacy. Kennedy demanded the immediate dismantling and removal of the missiles, and chose a naval blockade to prevent new missiles from arriving on the Caribbean island. The United States would intercept and inspect any ships believed to be carrying weapons, and members of the Organization of American States supported this action.

For several tense days during the Cuban missile crisis, Kennedy and Soviet Premier Nikita Khrushchev communicated through diplomatic channels. The world held its breath for fear of nuclear war between the superpowers. The crisis was solved after the Soviets agreed to remove the missiles and allow U.S. onsite inspection in return for the guarantee not to invade the island nation. Kennedy accepted, agreed to remove U.S. missiles from Turkey, and suspended the blockade, but Cuba refused to permit the promised inspection, out of anger at Soviet submission. Aerial photography did reveal that the missile bases were being dismantled. The entire incident revealed the young president's grace under extreme pressure. Kennedy had needed to redress the humiliation of the Bay of Pigs.

SEVEN SECONDS IN DALLAS

As Kennedy faced an uncertain re-election campaign, he began to pool support from those who could help. That meant traveling where his base was dwindling. Texas, home to Vice President Lyndon Johnson, was one of those areas. On November 22, 1963, Mrs. Kennedy, the vice president, and Mrs. Johnson, along with Governor John B. Connally of Texas and his wife, accompanied President Kennedy on a visit to Dallas, Texas. En route to a downtown luncheon, the president chose to ride in an open convertible through the motorcade route with his wife sitting beside him.

As the motorcade approached an underpass, shots rang out in rapid succession. President Kennedy slumped into his seat. One bullet passed through the president's neck and struck Governor Connally in the back. To everyone's horror, the next shot hit Kennedy in the head. Rushed to Parkland Memorial Hospital, the president never regained consciousness. Governor Connally survived surgery, and Vice President Lyndon Johnson, who had ridden two cars behind in the motorcade, was sworn in as president before the entourage flew back to Washington that day.

SUSPECT APPREHENDED

Hours later, Dallas police arrested the suspect Lee Harvey Oswald, an employee in a warehouse building along the motorcade route, who was also charged with shooting a police officer the same afternoon. Oswald's background check quickly revealed he'd suffered a troubled youth, defected to the Soviet Union (where he was denied citizenship), and had obvious Communist leanings.

Somewhere There Is a Conspiracy

Following the president's death numerous theories sprang up about whether there had been a conspiracy to commit the murder. Among those who were alleged at various points to have taken place in the plot were the CIA, the FBI, the NSA, the Soviets, the Cubans, the Mob, Lyndon Johnson, and Richard Nixon. Despite half a century of investigation, no definitive proof of a conspiracy has ever been produced.

Two days later, as the nation mourned the slain president and prepared for a state funeral, Oswald was himself assassinated while being transferred from one jail to another. Dallas nightclub owner Jack Ruby sprang from a group of reporters to shoot the suspect, who also died at Parkland Memorial Hospital. Chief Justice Earl Warren headed a special commission to investigate Kennedy's death and concluded in 1964 that Oswald had acted alone. In 1979, a committee from the U.S. House of Representatives acknowledged the possibility that a second assassin had been involved, and to this day, the Kennedy assassination is the subject of conspiracy theories and much debate. Jack Ruby was convicted of Oswald's death and later died in prison. The twenty-six-second home movie that Abraham Zapruder filmed when he stood in Dealey Plaza in Dallas, Texas, waiting for President John F. Kennedy's motorcade to pass by, is the graphic and gruesome accounting of the assassination that has been repeatedly studied and analyzed to try to understand what exactly happened.

NATIONAL MOURNING

On November 24, 1963, the nation mourned as the president's body was carried by horse-drawn carriage from the White House to the Rotunda of the Capitol. Hundreds of thousands filed past the coffin to pay their respects. A state funeral took place the next day. Foreign dignitaries and heads of state attended. Citizens lined the streets of Washington, D.C., as the funeral cortege made its way to Arlington National Cemetery. One poignant moment the nation would not soon forget was the sight of the slain president's three-year-old son, John Jr., saluting his father's casket. At Arlington, Mrs. Kennedy lit an eternal flame that still burns today. Jacqueline Kennedy Onassis was buried decades later next to her late husband.

VIETNAM

Quagmire in the Making

In the nineteenth century, France annexed the southeast Asian nation of Vietnam, placing it under colonial rule. In 1921, however, the revolutionary Ho Chi Minh created a nationalist party seeking independence from France. During World War II, the Japanese wrested control temporarily from the French, and as Japanese forces surrendered, Ho Chi Minh launched a full-scale revolt, taking Hanoi, the capital.

France refused to allow the independence movement, and by 1946 re-established rule, fearing (along with the United States) that all of Asia could become Communist as China fell to Mao Zedong. President Truman sent military supplies and funds for the French war in Vietnam, aiming to stem Communist imperialism. A ceasefire in July 1954 established a buffer zone between North and South Vietnam. The Communists, led by Ho Chi Minh, controlled the North, while Ngo Dinh Diem stepped in as interim premier in the south.

U.S. INVOLVEMENT BEGINS

Having seen enough war through the Korean conflict, Eisenhower was content to leave the area to itself, but as his successor took office, Communist forces were becoming more aggressive, carrying out attacks against South Vietnam. South Korea sent military advisors and aid to assist South Vietnam. Diem's regime, however, was corrupt, complicating matters for the United States as Vietcong

Communists within South Vietnam killed Diem's officials. General Maxwell Taylor, one of Kennedy's top advisors, suggested that sending a few thousand soldiers would quickly take care of the situation, and after Vice President Johnson returned from a fact-finding mission, he concurred that the United States needed to act against the Communist threat in Southeast Asia. Kennedy withdrew support of Diem's regime. Shortly thereafter, the Vietnamese overthrew and murdered Diem.

Following Kennedy's own assassination, President Johnson was wary of committing U.S. forces, but when North Vietnamese torpedo boats allegedly attacked U.S. naval destroyers in the Gulf of Tonkin, Johnson ordered immediate retaliation.

The Gulf of Tonkin Incident

Although at the time Lyndon Johnson used the apparent attack of a North Vietnamese boat on a U.S. destroyer to justify escalating U.S. presence in Vietnam, later investigation cast doubt on whether the North Vietnamese really attacked or whether radar blips confused naval personnel. However, this questioning occurred only after Congress passed the Gulf of Tonkin Resolution, authorizing Johnson to wage war in Indochina with whatever force he desired. By the end of 1964, approximately 20,000 troops had already been sent to the region.

THE LEAST-POPULAR WAR WAGED ON

The United States began a bombing campaign, code-named Operation Rolling Thunder, to stem the stream of supplies from Communist North Vietnam. But by 1965, when it became clear that mere bombing wasn't enough, the United States sent ground combat troops. Helicopter-borne troops surprised villages harboring suspected Communist supporters. Troops often destroyed such villages, forcing the Vietnamese to find new homes. Fighting became more brutal, as the Vietcong and the North Vietnamese were experts at mine warfare and guerrilla warfare.

In 1968, U.S. troops massacred Vietnamese civilians at the hamlet of My Lai in the aftermath of the Tet Offensive in Saigon (during which Vietcong soldiers attacked the U.S. embassy as well as multiple military targets throughout South Vietnam). At home, protests raged. Too many were dying for a cause not clearly defined or valued. Antiwar protests during the 1968 Democratic National Convention in Chicago provoked a riot by the city's police force.

The objections to the war were so profound that they convinced President Lyndon Johnson not to seek re-election in 1968. By 1969, hundreds of thousands of people were assembling in massive demonstrations, calling for the U.S. to withdraw its troops. In 1970, during a demonstration against the Vietnam War at Kent State University in Ohio, National Guardsmen fired into a crowd of students, killing four and wounding nine. The incident sparked a nationwide student strike, shutting down hundreds of universities.

The Vietnam Veterans Memorial

Visitors to Washington, D.C., can visit the Vietnam Veterans Memorial. The walls of the memorial are a deep black granite and form a V, deepest in the earth at the vertex, tapering and rising to ground level over their length of nearly 500 feet. The memorial is a moving tribute to Vietnam veterans, listing the names of 58,249 Americans who perished in the war.

Peace negotiations opened in Paris in May 1968, and after Richard Nixon won the presidential election, he began a gradual withdrawal of forces, which had reached a high of 550,000. Congress withdrew the Gulf of Tonkin Resolution on December 31, 1970, and a formal peace treaty was signed in 1973. The last U.S. combat troops left South Vietnam that March, and many prisoners of war were freed. In spite of the truce, skirmishes continued in South Vietnam, Cambodia, and Laos. The North Vietnamese troops entered Saigon as remaining Americans and South Vietnamese troops evacuated. South Vietnam's president announced an unconditional surrender in April 1975.

THE SPACE RACE

Aiming for the Stars

The Soviet launch of *Sputnik* in the 1950s and cosmonaut Yuri Gagarin's outer space journey in 1961 shifted Americans' attention to mastering space technology before the Russians did. The National Aeronautics and Space Administration (NASA) had already been created in 1958, but President Kennedy poured funding into the agency for research and space exploration. Project Mercury recruited seven brave pilots to become the first astronauts, and soon launched Alan Shepard as the first American in space, followed by John Glenn's 1962 achievement as the first American to orbit Earth. The *Telstar 1* satellite became the first telephone and television satellite as well.

Breaking the Sound Barrier

Test pilot and U.S. Air Force officer Chuck Yeager was the first aviator to fly faster than the speed of sound in 1947, maneuvering his plane (the *Glamorous Glennis*) through the shock waves produced as the plane neared the speed of Mach 1. Interestingly, because of the Cold War atmosphere at the time, Yeager's achievement was kept under wraps for some months.

The Apollo program carried on this tradition of achievement. On July 21, 1969, Neil Armstrong and "Buzz" Aldrin realized Kennedy's dream. Crewman Michael Collins watched as his fellow astronauts landed on and explored the lunar surface. "That's one small step for man, one giant leap for mankind," said Armstrong as he set foot on the moon, to a television audience watching in amazement at this great human achievement. Ten more astronauts explored the moon before the Apollo program ended in 1972. Space exploration turned to sending unmanned missions to other planets, a joint Soviet-American venture in space, and the manned space shuttle missions.

Kennedy Space Center

Following the president's death and cognizant of his quest for space exploration, NASA renamed its space center, on a promontory in eastern Florida known as Cape Canaveral, the John F. Kennedy Space Center. Today, visitors can watch satellite and space flight launches, view an IMAX presentation, take tours, and learn about America's space program.

THE *CHALLENGER* AND *COLUMBIA* DISASTERS

Beginning in 1981, the United States began experimenting with a reusable space vehicle, the space shuttle. Operational flights began in 1981 and continued for thirty years, conducting a variety of experiments in outer space, carrying supplies to the International Space Station (launched in 1998). Five operational shuttles were built:

- *Challenger*
- *Columbia*
- *Discovery*
- *Atlantis*
- *Endeavor*

On January 28, 1986, the shuttle *Challenger* was due to launch. Among the crew was Christa McAuliffe, a schoolteacher from New Hampshire, riding along as a payload specialist.

Seventy-three seconds after the launch, observers saw the shuttle disappear in a plume of white smoke. Debris fell into the ocean, and the horrified witnesses realized what they had seen was the shuttle exploding in midair. All seven crew members aboard were killed. Later investigation determined that the cause of the accident was the failure of an O-ring on the shuttle's booster rocket. There had been some concern about the O-rings but the issue was never properly addressed.

Seventeen years later, as the shuttle *Columbia* entered Earth's atmosphere after completing its mission it lost contact with Mission Control. A few minutes later, observers on the ground saw debris. The shuttle had broken apart, killing the crew of seven.

A subsequent investigation found that during the launch of the shuttle, it had been damaged by a large piece of foam that had broken loose. This created problems with the vehicle's wing, which came apart during re-entry.

THE COUNTERCULTURE

The Age of Aquarius

The 1960s were a decade of enormous social change. In many respects, the unpopular Vietnam War served as the catalyst for a counterculture movement in which young people openly questioned the status quo and decisions made by older generations. The birth control pill, which was introduced in 1960, gained popularity as well, leading to a sexual revolution and a change in lifestyle for many. By 1973, about 10 million women were using the "pill."

There were other factors as well. Many young people felt alienated by a society that increasingly seemed regimented and indifferent to the needs of the individual. In reaction, youth in the sixties rejected conformity and the advice of their elders. "Don't trust anyone over thirty," became the watchword of the day.

Some of those who dropped out of traditional society were called "hippies," and they gravitated to areas such as the Haight-Ashbury section of San Francisco. They became known as "flower children" because they believed in peace, love, and nature.

The Summer of Love

In the summer of 1967 thousands of young people traveled to San Francisco from all over the world and the hippie counterculture movement came into public awareness. The Human Be-In (modeled on the sit-in) in San Francisco's Golden Gate Park is said to have started the Summer of Love.

In August of 1969, more than 300,000 young people gathered at Max Yasgur's dairy farm in the small Catskills town of Bethel, New York, for the Woodstock Music & Art Fair.

Jimi Hendrix

Among those who performed at Woodstock was Jimi Hendrix, a musician from Seattle, known for his elaborate solos on electric guitar. During the concert, Hendrix played a rendition of "The Star Spangled Banner," using extensive amplifier feedback and distortion. Though some conservative critics denounced it as "un-American," others saw it as a statement about the contemporary United States.

Youth also experimented with mind-altering, illegal drugs such as LSD. The movement found its expression in alternative newspapers such as the *Chicago Seed* and the *Village Voice*, which promoted radical ideas. People such as Abbie Hoffman and Jerry Rubin led the counterculture, and musicians such as the Beatles also contributed. They were disciples of transcendental meditation (Eastern religions caught on in force during the decade), and after John Lennon married Yoko Ono, the unconventional pair decided to host a "bed-in for peace" for their honeymoon. They stayed in the presidential suite of a large Amsterdam hotel for seven days, protesting the war.

SIXTIES SENSATIONS

From movies such as *Dr. No*, marking the debut of Sean Connery as James Bond, 007, early in the decade to the rise of Motown recording stars, Americans enjoyed a vast array of entertainment. Berry Gordy Jr., an African American who made Motown Records of Detroit, Michigan, the most profitable minority business of its time, also built the fortunes and fame of artists such as Stevie Wonder, the Temptations, the Four Tops, Smokey Robinson and the Miracles, and Diana Ross and the Supremes. Successful musicians like these showed by example that blacks could achieve stardom. Their achievements helped break down the racial divide in America.

As the 1960s continued, folk music carried with it songs of protest with a sense of growing militancy against the war in Vietnam. Peter, Paul and Mary, Joan Baez, and Bob Dylan caught on with their music and their message. But there was also more traditional music. In 1966, *The Sound of Music* won an Academy Award for best film, with Julie Andrews, fresh from her recent success with *Mary Poppins*.

The Times Are A-Changin'

Bob Dylan's third album, *The Times They Are A-Changin'*, seemed to sum up the mood of rebellion and turmoil. The final lines of the title song captured it perfectly: "And the first one now / Will later be last. / For the times they are a-changin'."

MORE SIXTIES POP CULTURE

In sports, U.S. boxer Cassius Clay, who would later be known as Muhammad Ali when he became a Muslim, won the world heavyweight title. Andy Warhol startled the art world with pop art, a whole new style evident in images of Campbell's Soup Cans. And in the

1960s, being fashionable meant wearing false eyelashes, Vidal Sassoon hairstyles, and miniskirts as the rail-thin model Twiggy displayed so well. Knee- or thigh-high boots completed the fashion ensemble.

Television captured America's attention in this decade, turning the world into a virtual global village. Sporting events were increasingly broadcast.

What's on TV?

Comedies and talk shows aired at night, and the networks broadcast events such as the landing on the moon. Space exploration of the fictional variety could be seen with the starship *Enterprise*, as the show *Star Trek* launched in 1966 with characters Captain James Kirk and Mr. Spock boldly going where no man (and Vulcan) had gone before.

Two lasting icons for children's television began in the 1960s. When Fred Rogers began working at NBC in the 1950s, he knew there had to be a way to make a difference using this new medium. So when educational television began in his home area of Pittsburgh, Pennsylvania, Rogers left a promising career to begin his life's work. *Mister Rogers' Neighborhood* began airing in the United States in 1968. The next year, *Sesame Street*, funded by the Children's Television Workshop, quickly took hold with characters such as Big Bird, Cookie Monster, and Kermit the Frog, helping children everywhere learn their letters, numbers, and social skills.

WOMEN'S LIBERATION

Breaking the Glass Ceiling

During the 1970s and 1980s, the women's liberation movement surged forward. During the late 1960s, abortion became the topic of debate in the political arena. "Pro-choice" advocates believed that only a woman and her doctor should decide whether to end a pregnancy. They argued that life begins when the fetus can survive on its own outside the mother's womb. "Pro-life" advocates argued that life begins at conception and that states should prohibit the procedure. Many women had illegal abortions, risking their health and their lives. In 1973, however, the U.S. Supreme Court ruled in the case of *Roe v. Wade* that the state cannot restrict a woman's right to an abortion during the first trimester, the state can regulate the abortion procedure during the second trimester "in ways that are reasonably related to maternal health," and in the third trimester a state can choose to restrict or even to proscribe abortion as it sees fit.

Ms.

Gloria Steinem, a writer and political activist, cofounded the magazine *Ms.* in 1971 and women everywhere began insisting on the title Ms. as opposed to Miss or Mrs., asserting that the courtesy title of their male counterparts (Mr.) did not reveal their marital status.

Religious and conservative groups led the outcry against the Supreme Court's decision. They also categorized women who supported the proposed Equal Rights Amendment (ERA) as immoral and antifamily. They sent an underlying message that played on hidden fears that if the ERA passed, America would see same-sex marriages and unisex bathrooms. Yet women who felt they could rise only so far (to the "glass ceiling") in a male-dominated corporate world argued for equal pay for equal work. Betty Friedan, Gloria Steinem, Bella Abzug, and Shirley Chisholm, among others, argued for agendas including childcare centers and equal opportunities in employment, education, and in the military, as well as abortion rights.

Key Feminist Texts

- *The Feminine Mystique* by Betty Friedan
- *The Second Sex* by Simone de Beauvoir
- *Fear of Flying* by Erica Jong
- *The Female Eunuch* by Germaine Greer
- *The Dialectic of Sex* by Shulamith Firestone

By August 1974, the Equal Rights Amendment had been ratified by thirty-three of the required thirty-eight states. A congressional mandate had set March 1979 as the deadline for ratification, and by June 1978, only three additional states had approved the ERA. Even when given an extension for approval, the amendment failed to be ratified. Yet many states now do guarantee equality of the sexes in their state constitutions.

WOMEN AND ELECTIVE OFFICE

The numbers of women elected to various offices increased steadily throughout the second half of the twentieth century. In 1964 Margaret Chase Smith, a Republican, became the first woman to run for a major party presidential nomination. Eight years later, Democrat Shirley Chisholm became the first to run for the Democratic nomination; she was also the first African American to do so. In the 1984 presidential race, Democratic candidate Walter Mondale chose as his running mate Rep. Geraldine Ferraro, making her the first woman on a major party presidential ticket. (Mondale and Ferraro lost to Ronald Reagan and George H.W. Bush.)

Since then, other women have run for the nation's top political offices, including Republican vice presidential candidate Sarah Palin (2008) and Democratic presidential candidate Sen. Hillary Clinton (2008). Clinton subsequently served as secretary of state in the administration of Barack Obama, the second woman to hold that position (the first was Madeleine Albright in 1997 during the presidency of Bill Clinton).

ENVIRONMENTALISM

Saving the Earth

On April 22, 1970, across the United States tens of thousands of people participated in demonstrations and other actions advocating environmental reform. Awareness of the need for environmental activism had been steadily growing, and Earth Day, as it came to be known, offered an opportunity to show it.

SILENT SPRING

One of the most important turning points in environmental consciousness came in 1962 with the publication of Rachel Carson's *Silent Spring*. Carson, a marine biologist, had been concerned since the 1940s with the effects of pesticides, particularly DDT, on the environment. In her book, Carson reported on the devastation caused by the introduction of artificial chemicals into the environment—the wholesale death of birds and animals and the disruption of the delicate balance of what became known as the ecosystem.

Although various presidents (particularly Theodore Roosevelt) had attempted to preserve parts of the American environment, the 1970s and 1980s marked a time of renewed government and popular interest in reducing pollution and making better use of natural resources. Among the steps taken were:

- Passage of the Endangered Species Act (1973)
- Amendments to the Clean Air Act (1970)
- Amendments to the Clean Water Act (1977)

Concerns were also raised about global warming and population control, particularly in Paul Ehrlich and David Brower's 1970 bestseller *The Population Bomb*. Although some of the catastrophic consequences they predicted did not come to pass, people became more conscious of the need to make more efficient use of environmental resources.

GLOBAL WARMING

Around 2000, many scientists increased their warnings about the effects of global warming. In particular, former vice president Al Gore, through his documentary film *An Inconvenient Truth*, sounded the alarm about climate change and a general rise in global temperatures.

Possible Effects of Global Warming

- Polar ice caps melt
- Ocean levels rise, flooding many coastal communities
- Increase in extreme events such as hurricanes and superstorms
- Spreading droughts, leading to food shortages

By the end of the first decade of the twenty-first century, scientific consensus had coalesced around the dangers of global warming and the need for governmental policies to combat it.

WATERGATE

Cancer in the Presidency

On June 17, 1972, Washington, D.C., police were startled when they captured five men breaking into the Democratic National Committee (DNC) offices at the Watergate apartment and office complex. The men, who carried bugging equipment, also had large amounts of cash and were dressed in business suits.

The Watergate Burglars

1. Virgilio González
2. Bernard Barker
3. Frank Sturgis
4. Eugenio Martinez
5. James McCord

Investigation revealed they had ties to a White House secret unit collectively known as the "Plumbers," given the name for their ability to plug White House information leaks. As history would record, however, their duties extended to spying and other odd jobs.

The DNC office break-in targeted the Democratic Party leader Larry O'Brien Jr., who had connections dating back to the 1960 election that Nixon had lost to Kennedy. The two *Washington Post* journalists assigned to cover this story—dubbed a "third-rate burglary" by the White House—were Bob Woodward and Carl Bernstein. As they gathered clues, the two pieced together a trail of money and cover-ups that led back to the Committee to Re-Elect the President (CREEP) and to the Oval Office. U.S. District Court Judge John

Sirica, in whose court the burglars were arraigned, remained persistent in his questioning, which also helped crack the case.

Deep Throat

Although Woodward and Bernstein used many sources to put together their stories, one in particular supplied them with valuable inside information. For nearly thirty-three years, the identity of this source was keep secret and known only as "Deep Throat." On May 31, 2005, W. Mark Felt Sr., who retired in 1973 as the United States Federal Bureau of Investigation's number two official, revealed himself to be the Watergate scandal whistleblower.

Despite the growing scandal, Nixon won re-election in 1972 by an overwhelming majority. However, behind the scenes tensions grew within his administration as Woodward and Bernstein and others slowly converged on the truth.

A Senate committee on the Watergate scandal convened, as did an investigation by special prosecutor Archibald Cox. These investigations shed light on the espionage conducted against Nixon's political rivals. With each revelation, it seemed as if one more official in the Nixon administration was forced out or resigned. After the resignation of Nixon's two top aides, H.R. Haldeman and John Ehrlichman, it became clear that the presidential inner circle was implicated in the Watergate scandal.

When it was disclosed that the president routinely taped Oval Office conversations, investigators had the tool they needed to chip away at the deception and reveal the truth. Yet President Nixon, claiming executive privilege, refused to hand over the tapes. He viewed them as his personal property. When he supplied heavily edited transcripts instead, the special prosecutor appealed to the Supreme Court. In July 1974, the court ordered Nixon to give up the tapes.

Saturday Night Massacre

In October 1973, Nixon ordered the special prosecutor, Archibald Cox, not to request any more tapes. Cox refused to do this, and Nixon commanded Attorney General Elliot Richardson to fire Cox. Richardson refused and resigned, whereupon Nixon ordered the number two man at the Justice Department, William Ruckelshaus, to fire Cox. Ruckelshaus also refused and resigned. Finally Robert Bork, the solicitor general, carried out the firing.

The events were known as the Saturday Night Massacre and caused a massive loss of support for Nixon. The president was subsequently forced to appoint a new special prosecutor, Leon Jaworski, to continue the investigation of the Watergate scandal.

THE FALL OF A PRESIDENT

In October 1973, the House Judiciary Committee began considering impeachment proceedings against Nixon, who was stalling with the subpoenaed material. In July 1974, the House voted to introduce three impeachment articles charging Nixon with obstructing justice, abusing presidential power, and refusing to obey subpoenas from the House of Representatives.

On August 5, bowing to pressure, Nixon released tapes that clearly showed his involvement in the Watergate cover-up as early as June 1972. The tape that did the most damage, recorded on June 23, became known as "the smoking gun" and recorded the president planning to use the CIA to impede the FBI's investigation of the burglary.

What little support remained for President Nixon quickly eroded. House impeachment and Senate conviction seemed certain. After a visit from Republican leader Barry Goldwater and others, Nixon announced that he would resign from office. On August 9, 1974, he flew away from the White House in a helicopter, and shortly thereafter, Vice President Gerald R. Ford was sworn in as president, inheriting a nation in shock and dismay at the problems in their government. Ford was the first vice president and the first president to ascend to both positions without being elected to either of those offices.

AFTERMATH OF WATERGATE

Richard Nixon never admitted guilt over the Watergate affair, (although in a television interview with David Frost he said he had "let down" the American people) and historians believe that if it were not for the man's suspicion, smear campaigns, and illicit activities, his presidency would have been remembered for its foreign policy strides rather than for scandal.

In September 1974, President Ford issued a pardon to Nixon for all federal crimes he may have committed during his administration. It was an unpopular decision and may have cost Ford re-election in 1976. Yet it spared the nation a great deal of lingering turmoil.

In the wake of Watergate, citizens remained distrustful, and government officials and politicians had to earn back that trust. Reflecting national skepticism, journalists began digging into candidates' past behaviors.

In his retirement, Richard Nixon wrote books on political affairs, including *No More Vietnams* (1985), *In the Arena* (1990), and *Beyond Peace* (1994). Nixon traveled and gradually regained some respect for his foreign policy expertise. He died of a stroke in 1994 and was buried next to his wife, Pat, on the grounds of his presidential library.

RONALD REAGAN

The New Conservatism

In 1980, the presidential race pitted the incumbent chief executive, Jimmy Carter, against a newcomer to national politics, Ronald Reagan. First well known as an actor and later governor of California, Reagan charmed the public, and his conservative following in particular. The nation seemed to be searching for old-fashioned values, and voters found them in Ronald Reagan.

THE GREAT COMMUNICATOR

As the Carter administration failed to revive a sagging economy, Americans looked to Reagan for leadership. He'd previously tried to enter the national political arena (challenging Gerald Ford for the Republican nomination in 1976), but this time people took Ronald Reagan more seriously. In an ironic twist, Reagan briefly considered former president Ford as a potential running mate, but selected George H.W. Bush instead.

Reagan blasted Carter on the campaign trail on everything from the struggling economy to the need for a strong military.

In Iran, a fundamentalist religious movement seized power, installing the Ayatollah Khomeini as the supreme ruler of the Islamic state. In 1979 a group of radical Iranian students took over the U.S. embassy in Tehran, holding fifty-two diplomats and staffers hostage.

The Iranian hostage crisis dragged on through the closing year of the Carter administration. Each day, programs such as ABC's *Nightline* kept the drama alive for Americans. The Iranian stalemate humiliated the nation. Failure to resolve it contributed to Ronald Reagan's defeat of Carter in the presidential election. After the election, with the assistance of Algerian intermediaries, successful negotiations began. On January 20, 1981, the day of President Reagan's inauguration, the United States released almost $8 billion in Iranian assets and the hostages were freed after 444 days in Iranian detention. The agreement also gave Iran immunity from lawsuits arising from the incident.

Argo

Unbeknownst to the Iranians, a small group of Americans escaped the embassy and took refuge in the Canadian embassy. They remained hidden there until they were smuggled out of the country in an elaborate CIA plot. The agency pretended the Americans were actually a Canadian film crew making a science fiction movie titled *Argo*.

The story was told in the 2012 film *Argo*, which won the Academy Award for best picture.

REAGAN TAKES THE HELM

Reagan brought sweeping change to the economy and social policies that had been set in place over the preceding decades. He reduced federal programs and lifted restrictions on business activities and regulations. Conservative and religious groups, businesses in search of tax breaks and eased restrictions, and defense contractors wanting a piece of Reagan's new military buildup supported the president's agenda. So did those who believed the USSR was the proverbial U.S. enemy. Televangelist Jerry Falwell had a very public pulpit with his Moral Majority, pressing for prayer in public schools and restrictions on abortion, gay rights, and women's rights.

Death of an Idol

On December 8, 1980, John Lennon was shot to death by a deranged fan outside his Manhattan apartment building. After returning home from a recording session with his wife, Yoko Ono, Lennon stepped from his limousine and was shot twice by Mark David Chapman. A section of Central Park was named Strawberry Fields in honor of John Lennon in 1981.

On March 31, 1981, Reagan's presidency was almost cut short by an assassination attempt. His attacker, John W. Hinckley Jr., was an unstable drifter acting out a fantasy to gain the attention of actress Jodie Foster. Foster had costarred in the movie *Taxi Driver*, which partly dealt with political assassination. Hinckley was found not guilty by reason of insanity and committed to a mental hospital. Reagan recovered from the shooting, although later accounts made clear that his abilities were greatly diminished, especially during his second term. The public's concern and support made it a bit easier for the new president to push through his legislative agenda.

REAGANOMICS

The recession that had begun during the previous decade lingered, but during the 1980s, economic recovery began. Inflation was low, but with interest rates at record highs, many wealthy citizens prospered as a result of "Reaganomics." This was an era of conspicuous consumption by "yuppies," young urban professionals, and members of the upper class. However, the effect was to further increase the gap between rich and poor.

As well, government spending and a burgeoning civil service produced a record national debt, which future generations would have to contend with. In October 1987, Wall Street investors panicked, causing stocks to plummet 508 points, even more sharply than they'd done in 1929. However, the nation did not slump into a depression, but recovered from "Black Monday."

Still, thousands of manufacturing jobs were eliminated in the new economy and replaced with lower-paying positions in service industries. Poverty became more of a problem with cuts in many social services that would have helped those who most needed assistance. The emphasis was clearly on the supply side of economics, with the hope that money would trickle down from the top.

REAGAN'S FOREIGN POLICY

If détente (peaceful coexistence) had been stressed in the prior decade, in the 1980s it was de-emphasized in favor of fighting Communist influences. Much of this fighting occurred in Central America and in the Caribbean. The United States cut off aid to Nicaragua in order to support an anti-Sandinista guerrilla movement known as the Contras. Nicaragua signed an aid pact with the Soviet Union, and Reagan focused on sending money, weapons, and military training to the Contras, as well as arms and advisors to El Salvador. In addition, the United States claimed that it was not bound by the jurisdiction of the International Court of Justice regarding the alleged illegality of the mining of the Nicaraguan harbors.

In 1983, U.S. troops invaded Grenada, a Caribbean island, after rebels overthrew the government there. (Some critics argued that the real purpose of the Grenada invasion had been to overcome "Vietnam Syndrome," that is, a reluctance to use U.S. military power abroad.) Reagan supported anti-Marxist regimes in Afghanistan and Angola. Unlike Vietnam, the fighting brought few casualties. In the Middle East, the president wasn't as lucky: U.S. Marines were attacked in their Beirut headquarters after Reagan sent them into Lebanon to strengthen the Christian government, and 248 were killed. Even after the president pulled the marines out of the territory, radical Muslims kidnapped many Westerners.

The Teflon Presidency

Known as the "Teflon president" because none of his mistakes seemed to stick, Reagan won re-election in 1984 against his Democratic opponent, Walter Mondale. Democrats slowly gained control in Congress, which made legislative initiatives difficult for President Reagan as his tenure neared an end.

The country's armed forces buildup contributed to keeping the Soviets in check. The military boasted of its Strategic Defense Initiative technology, often called "Star Wars," which was supposed to permit the United States to intercept enemy missiles before they hit their targets. Reagan had insisted on the technology, though many felt it was too expensive and unreliable. The U.S. rearmament brought much protest from Mikhail Gorbachev, the Soviet leader, during summit meetings. However, the two superpower leaders agreed to eliminate land-based nuclear missiles of intermediate and shorter range. These were admittedly only a small fraction of both nations' nuclear arsenals, but nonetheless it was progress in the arms race.

IRAN-CONTRA

A Secret Policy Unravels

During his second term, Ronald Reagan's administration became embroiled in controversy, damaging his reputation as an honest communicator. In November 1986, word leaked to newspapers that the United States had secretly sold weapons to Iran, diverting approximately $30 million in profits from these sales to help the Contras fight the leftist Sandinista government in Nicaragua. If indeed arms had been swapped for hostages, it would embarrass the administration, for once the arms were in Iranian control, others could use them to capture additional hostages. But the matter was even more complex.

Initially, Reagan denied the allegations that arms had been swapped to win the release of U.S. hostages held by terrorists (who supported Iran). Administration sources blamed the diversion of profits on Lieutenant Colonel Oliver North, a National Security Council staff member who directed the secret operations against Nicaragua. North had set up covert support for the Contras, including airplanes and secret bank accounts. He had reported his activities initially to his superior, National Security Advisor Robert C. McFarlane, and subsequently to McFarlane's successor, Admiral John Poindexter. Congressional hearings focused on whether and how Reagan was personally involved in the matter, and particularly whether his administration violated the Boland amendments forbidding U.S. military aid to the Contras. North denied the administration's claims that he'd acted independently. To complicate matters for the White House, North had a certain All-American patriotic fervor about him that appealed to people, making his testimony all the more believable.

Let Them Eat Cake

In one of the more farcical moments of the Iran-Contra affair, in 1986, with Reagan's approval, Robert McFarlane made a trip to Tehran to negotiate with what he and the president believed were "moderates" in the Iranian government. McFarlane brought with him a Bible, personally inscribed by Reagan, and a cake. The Iranians, apparently, were less than impressed.

Admiral John Poindexter testified that he'd never told Reagan about the diversion of funds, but that the president had approved a direct arms-for-hostages deal with Iran. In the end, members of Congress admonished the administration for its incompetence in handling the secret operations and funding. But there was no overall investigation of Contras financing, for the investigative committee found no concrete evidence to suggest that Reagan had known of the diversion of funds to the Contras. Oliver North was tried and convicted in 1989 of obstructing Congress and unlawfully destroying government documents, but his conviction was later reversed. Poindexter was also found guilty, and this verdict was also overturned.

Arms and Drugs?

It had been alleged that there were ties between the Contras and drug smugglers—this in an era when the first lady had publicly espoused a campaign for schoolchildren called "Just Say No" to drugs.

Reagan, in an unusual move for a president, agreed to appear before a congressional committee investigating the affair. However, his testimony was marked by contradictions (he at first said he'd approved trading arms for hostages, then denied it) and by constant repetition that he didn't remember details. To many, the testimony indicated a president seriously out of touch with the actions of his administration.

Just when everyone thought the matter was put to rest, it resurfaced for George Bush when he issued pardons for many high-level government officials charged or convicted of Iran-Contra activities. Independent prosecutor Lawrence E. Walsh issued a final report on the investigation in January 1994. He found no evidence that President Reagan had broken the law but admitted that Reagan may have known about or participated in a cover-up of the scandal.

END OF THE REAGAN ERA

Toward the end of Reagan's tenure as president, it was reported that he dozed off during cabinet meetings and spent less and less time on presidential duties. The Iran-Contra affair had weakened his political clout, and Congress openly rejected some of his initiatives. Congress overrode a presidential veto of a civil-rights enforcement bill and refused funding for Contras military operations.

But Reagan's successors, not the president himself, would have to address the government spending that had begun under the president dubbed "the Gipper."

THE COLLAPSE OF COMMUNISM

Parting the Iron Curtain

The Communist empire unexpectedly began to unravel during the tenure of Mikhail Gorbachev. He initiated a campaign called *perestroika* (Russian for "restructuring"), reforming and revitalizing the Soviet system that had been in place for decades. Gorbachev first mentioned his ideas in a speech before the Central Committee of the Communist Party in 1985, and his policy of *glasnost* ("openness") became the subject of public debate. Works previously banned were now published; the Soviet media was also less restricted.

Unfortunately, the Soviet economy was still hurting, and perestroika introduced a market-based system, encouraging private ownership, which had always been shunned by previous Communist regimes. Perestroika was far more than economic reform. The broader use of the term meant social, political, and most definitely historic change. Soviet citizens, for instance, would have a greater say in who would run their government.

Yet this sweeping change was not automatically welcomed. Youth, often better educated and largely dissatisfied with the traditional system, embraced the concepts, but the less educated, older generations opposed them. Under the new Soviet system, prices soared, as did unemployment. When people could get to the stores through the long lines, they often found nothing of value. Unable to navigate the change as the Soviet economy continued its decline, Gorbachev watched as the USSR collapsed in 1991 and Russia remained under the leadership of elected president Boris Yeltsin. Communist governments in Central and Eastern Europe also collapsed as a result.

The Wall Comes Down

As the Iron Curtain collapsed, one image captured the moment—the toppling of the Berlin Wall. An East German government statement broadcast on November 9, 1989, stated that the crossing of the border would be permitted. As East Germans crossed into West Germany, the first step of German reunification began. The wall was subsequently destroyed over a period of several weeks.

REDRAWING THE MAP

Yeltsin withstood an attempted coup that sought to reinstate officials of the Communist Party. However, he increasingly showed signs of alcoholism, and his tenure as Russian leader ended in confusion and disgrace. He was replaced by Prime Minister Vladimir Putin, who provided a strong—some said dictatorial—hand on the Russian government.

The collapse of the Soviet Union meant that the various states that had been part of it broke away and formed independent republics:

Former Soviet Republics

- Armenia
- Azerbaijan
- Georgia
- Kazakhstan
- Kyrgyzstan
- Tajikistan
- Turkmenistan
- Ukraine
- Uzbekistan

THE FIRST GULF WAR

Coalition in the Desert

Vice President George Herbert Walker Bush won the 1988 election against Democratic rival Michael Dukakis. However, his choice of Senator Dan Quayle, seen as a lightweight politician, as running mate made him fodder for late-night comedians, further eroding public confidence.

NO BEATING AROUND THE BUSH

Bush believed that the former Soviet Union could become an ally, and that if the Cold War ended, American taxpayers would no longer have to finance the military might it had necessitated. Thus, Bush helped edge the Soviet leader toward democracy. As the Berlin Wall separating Communist East Berlin from capitalist West Berlin fell in November 1989, Bush showed restraint rather than gloating over the event. He talked of "a new world order" to replace the former relations between the two superpowers.

Bush gravitated toward foreign affairs rather than many domestic initiatives.

REMOVING NORIEGA

In 1989, Manuel Noriega, the Panamanian leader indicted in the United States for drug trafficking, nullified a presidential election that had swept him out of power, even after U.S. observers insisted he had lost. Critics pointed to the fact that Noriega had been an agent of the Central Intelligence Agency (CIA) while President Bush had been the agency's director. Bush sent troops to Panama to assist in a coup against Noriega. The invasion lasted only days and resulted in Noriega's capture and return to the mainland, where he was convicted in Miami, Florida, on drug and racketeering charges in 1992.

TENSIONS IN THE PERSIAN GULF

Iraq, however, demanded much of Bush's attention as Iraqi leader Saddam Hussein launched an offensive on neighboring Kuwait in August 1990. The tiny nation, governed by a sheik, held 10 percent of the world's oil reserves. Saudi Arabia, home to another 25 percent of the world's reserves, bordered Saddam's forces. It was too close for comfort for many in the Western world. If Saddam Hussein, a headstrong leader at best, ordered another attack, he would control almost half of the world's oil.

President Bush favored diplomatic resolution of the tensions, but also vowed that Hussein would not succeed with his naked aggression. In a televised speech, Bush likened Hussein to Hitler. The president created a coalition under the auspices of the United Nations (UN), including many European, Asian, and Middle Eastern countries (some of whom had had their own tensions with one another). Bush convinced the Saudi Arabians to allow a U.S. troop presence on their soil. The U.S. Department of Defense deployed military weapons and soldiers, even some called up from the reserve forces, in the largest such undertaking since Vietnam.

Bush demonstrated patience when Arab nations (such as Egypt) bowed to political pressure to resolve the tensions alone. But when this failed, the Arabs joined the UN coalition along with Russia, a longtime ally of Iraq. Negotiations between Secretary of State James Baker and Iraqi foreign minister Tariq Aziz, and UN resolutions, continued while the president deployed the military. Despite Hussein's requests for a portion of Kuwait, Bush held firm to his demand for complete withdrawal and warned of the consequences if he was not heeded. The proverbial line in the sand was drawn with a deadline of January 15 for Hussein's withdrawal.

Congressional Approval

The United Nations Security Council had already sanctioned the use of force, if necessary, in 1990. President Bush received congressional approval for possible military action on January 16, 1991. He ordered the multinational invasion of Kuwait called Operation Desert Storm to begin the next day, January 17.

OPERATION DESERT STORM

The Allied coalition had approximately 1,700 aircraft poised to attack Iraqi forces. General Norman Schwarzkopf of the U.S. Army commanded the operation. Apache helicopter gunships and Stealth fighters went into service. Finally, the United States had a chance to use many of the weapons amassed during the Reagan-Bush era, including cruise missiles.

Though the Stealths were designed to be invisible to radar, the U.S. Air Force took no chances and jammed enemy radar. Unfortunately, the jamming alerted the Iraqis that something was happening, and Hussein ordered blind firing of missiles without even knowing the target. The Allied bombing destroyed much of Iraq's communications ability. The next targets were weapons factories where it was believed Hussein had stockpiled arsenals of biological and chemical weapons.

THE GROUND WAR

On February 24, the ground war began as U.S. Marines penetrated Iraqi lines and pushed to liberate Kuwait City. Kuwaiti oil fields were already ablaze, filling the skies with thick, black smoke. Again, Saddam Hussein ignored demands to withdraw from the country. The Allied air force kept attacking Iraqi tank positions, using all of its military might, including B-52s and bombers from the nuclear strike force. With laser-guided bombs, U.S. forces destroyed tank after tank. From the sea, the USS *Missouri* shelled the beach.

Fleeting Popularity

In the months after the Gulf War, President Bush enjoyed a 90 percent approval rating among Americans. As the months wore on to the 1992 election, however, it became evident that although Bush handled foreign relations well, his comprehension didn't extend to his electorate, who resented his inaction on domestic matters.

Critics felt the Allied effort didn't go far enough: it failed to eliminate Hussein altogether, or to press forward to take Baghdad. In his defense, Bush cited his original objective—to liberate Kuwait for its rightful government and leaders, not to remove any other leader such as Saddam Hussein. The president consulted with General Colin Powell, chairman of the Joint Chiefs of Staff, and they decided to end the war effort. Compared to other wars' casualty numbers, the Allied casualty count was relatively low: a total of 149 Allied soldiers died in the line of duty, and a little more than 500 were wounded. Iraqi casualties were much higher, with estimates ranging from 25,000 to 100,000.

9/11

Everything Is Different Now

The morning of September 11, 2001, was a spectacular fall day in the Northeast. At 8:45 A.M., as people were walking through the streets of downtown Manhattan, many of them on their way to the World Trade Center towers and office buildings near the towers, a hijacked passenger jet, American Airlines Flight 11 out of Boston's Logan Airport, crashed into the north tower of the World Trade Center, tearing a gaping hole in the building and setting it afire. As people watched the burning tower in horror, a second hijacked airliner, United Airlines Flight 175 from Boston, crashed into the south tower of the World Trade Center at 9:03 A.M. and exploded. Both buildings were now in flames. At approximately 9:43 A.M. American Airlines Flight 77 out of Washington exploded when it hit the Pentagon, killing all sixty-four people aboard. At 10:05 A.M. the south tower fell, sending a huge cloud of dust and debris through the streets of lower Manhattan. At 10:10 A.M. United Airlines Flight 93 out of Newark and bound for San Francisco, also hijacked, crashed in Somerset County, Pennsylvania, southeast of Pittsburgh, killing thirty-eight passengers, crew, and hijackers. At 10:28 A.M. the north tower of the World Trade Center collapsed. As it became apparent that terrorism was behind the attack, most realized that many things would no longer be the same.

OSAMA BIN LADEN AND AL-QAEDA

Shortly after the attacks of September 11, the terrorist group, Al-Qaeda, under the leadership of Osama bin Laden, was suspected of being responsible. Al-Qaeda has its origins in the uprising against the 1979 Soviet occupation of Afghanistan and was, ironically, the beneficiary of aid from the United States during that period.

After the Soviets left Afghanistan, bin Laden returned to his native Saudi Arabia and then later set up bases in Sudan in northeast Africa. In 1994 Sudan expelled bin Laden, who moved his base of operations to Afghanistan. Bin Laden was welcomed by the Taliban ("Students of Islamic Knowledge Movement") who came to power during Afghanistan's long civil war and ruled Afghanistan from 1996 until 2001.

Among the claims of Al-Qaeda, which resulted in bin Laden's declaration of war against the United States, were America's participation in the first Gulf War, United States military involvements in Somalia and Yemen, and the United States military presence in Saudi Arabia.

AMERICA'S REACTION

On September 20, 2001, President Bush addressed a joint session of Congress, members of the various branches of the national government, and the American people from the House of Representatives. He was quick to get to Al-Qaeda, bin Laden, and the hosting government, the Taliban:

"Tonight, the United States of America makes the following demands on the Taliban: Deliver to United States authorities all the leaders of Al-Qaeda who hide in your land. (Applause.) Release all foreign nationals, including American citizens, you have unjustly imprisoned. Protect foreign journalists, diplomats and aid workers in your country. Close immediately and permanently every terrorist training camp in Afghanistan, and hand over every terrorist, and every person in their support structure, to appropriate authorities. (Applause.) Give the United States full access to terrorist training camps, so we can make sure they are no longer operating.

"These demands are not open to negotiation or discussion. (Applause.) The Taliban must act, and act immediately. They will hand over the terrorists, or they will share in their fate."

Following the destruction of the Twin Towers in New York, plans were laid for the construction of a new World Trade Center next to the National September 11 Memorial & Museum, located on the same spot as the original towers in lower Manhattan.

THE AFGHAN AND IRAQ WARS

Fighting Terror Abroad

On October 7, 2001, after the Taliban failed to respond to America's demands to end its connections with Al-Qaeda, the United States, Great Britain, and coalition forces launched a bombing campaign against the Taliban government and terrorist camps in Afghanistan. Although the immediate goal was to destroy Al-Qaeda and capture bin Laden, the president stated that the "battle was broader." Within two months the Taliban government had fallen. Although Osama bin Laden was not caught, the Al-Qaeda forces in Afghanistan were seriously weakened.

Planning for Iraq

Memoirs by former members of the Bush administration have made it clear that immediately after the September 11 attacks, President Bush and Vice President Cheney began searching for a connection between the attacks and Saddam Hussein. Despite being repeatedly told that no such connection existed, Cheney continued to assert that the American invasion of Iraq was justified by Hussein's sponsorship of the 9/11 attackers.

THE PATRIOT ACT

Forty-five days after the September 11 attacks, Congress, with little if any debate, passed the 342-page USA PATRIOT Act (Uniting and

Strengthening America by Providing Appropriate Tools Required to Intercept and Obstruct Terrorism Act). The vote in the House of Representatives was 357 to 66 and in the Senate 98 to 1, with Senator Russ Feingold of Wisconsin being the only senator to vote against the act.

Search and Seizure

Section 213 of the USA Patriot Act contains the first authorization for the issuance of "sneak and peek" search warrants in American history. These warrants allow search and seizure without notifying the individual being searched at the time of the search. This section is not restricted to terrorists or terrorism offenses; it may be used in connection with any federal crime, including misdemeanors.

Included in the legislation were sections that provided:

- Domestic terrorism definitions and greater authority to subject political organizations to surveillance
- Greater powers to law authorities to conduct secret searches of phone, Internet, medical, banking, and student records with minimal judicial oversight
- Greater powers to conduct investigations of American citizens without probable cause if it's for "intelligence purposes"
- Power to incarcerate noncitizens for indefinite periods on mere suspicion with no right of counsel, habeas corpus, or opportunities to appear before public tribunals

Since its passage, nearly 200 cities/towns and three states have passed resolutions stating that the Patriot Act is not enforceable within their jurisdictions, claiming that among other concerns, the First, Fourth, Fifth, Sixth, Eighth, and Fourteenth Amendments are being threatened. The USA Patriot Act has raised the tension that exists when a country is at "war" and national security is pitted against civil liberties. The balance that must be maintained is the protection and security of society without sacrificing the very system that is being kept secure. Following successful constitutional challenges to some sections of the act, the Patriot Act was renewed in March 2006.

THE DEPARTMENT OF HOMELAND SECURITY

On November 25, 2002, President Bush signed into law legislation creating a new cabinet-level Department of Homeland Security. The new department would employ 170,000 people and combine all or part of twenty-two other agencies, including:

- Immigration and Naturalization
- Coast Guard
- Border Patrol

The creation of Homeland Security would bring the total number of departments to fifteen:

1. Agriculture
2. Commerce

3. Defense
4. Education
5. Energy
6. Health and Human Services
7. Homeland Security
8. Housing and Urban Development
9. Interior
10. Labor
11. State
12. Transportation
13. Treasury
14. Veterans Affairs
15. Office of the Attorney General

OPERATION IRAQI FREEDOM

Turning their attention from Afghanistan, the Bush administration began to publicly make the case for attacking Iraq. Officials strongly implied a connection between Saddam and the 9/11 attacks, though intelligence sources said no such connection existed.

In addition, the administration had a strong argument: Saddam, they argued, had arsenals of weapons of mass destruction. These might even include nuclear weapons.

False Trail

Among the evidence cited by officials of Saddam's nuclear program was the assertion by an informant that Iraqi agents had tried to buy "yellow cake" uranium in Africa. However, the informant turned out to be lying.

The culmination of the administration's pro-war campaign was a speech by Secretary of State Colin Powell before the United Nations Security Council in February 2003 in which he laid out the details of the Bush government's case. His speech received wide press coverage and general support.

The military invasion of Iraq was known as Operation Iraqi Freedom. These military operations would be against the state of Iraq to rid the country of its weapons of mass destruction and remove Saddam Hussein and his government from power. On February 26, 2003, President George W. Bush stated:

> The United States has no intention of determining the precise form of Iraq's new government. That choice belongs to the Iraqi people. Yet, we will ensure that one brutal dictator is not replaced by another. All Iraqis must have a voice in the new government, and all citizens must have their rights protected.
>
> Rebuilding Iraq will require a sustained commitment from many nations, including our own: we will remain in Iraq as long as necessary, and not a day more.

THE 2002 STATE OF THE UNION AND THE AXIS OF EVIL

In the heady days leading up to the invasion, the president denounced North Korea, Iran, and Iraq as an "axis of evil" and warned that the United States would wage war against countries developing weapons of mass destruction. There were parts of his State of the Union address that were later found to be untrue; for example, the president stated, "Our discoveries in Afghanistan confirmed our worst fears and showed us the true scope of the task ahead. We have found diagrams of American nuclear power plants."

The Outing of Valerie Plame

A prominent critic of the administration's war plans was former diplomat Joseph Wilson, who debunked the claim about Saddam trying to purchase uranium. In July 2003, a columnist for the *Washington Post* revealed in his column that Wilson's wife, Valerie Plame, was a CIA agent. This statement effectively ended Plame's career as a covert operative, and she and her husband blamed officials within the Bush administration for leaking her status as payback for her husband's criticism. Further investigations into the matter proved inconclusive.

On September 12, 2002, President Bush addressed the United Nations and called for "regime change" in Iraq. On October 11, 2002, Congress passed the Joint Resolution to Authorize the Use of United States Armed Forces Against Iraq. On November 8, 2002, the United Nations Security Council passed a unanimous resolution calling for tough new arms inspections and demanding that Iraq disarm or face serious consequences. This was followed by the return of United Nations weapons inspectors to Iraq for the first time in nearly four years. On December 7, 2002, Iraq submitted a statement on its chemical, biological, and nuclear capabilities, claiming it possessed no banned weapons.

DOUBTS ABOUT THE IRAQI WAR

On November 8, 2002, the United Nations Security Council passed a unanimous resolution calling on Iraq to disarm or face "serious consequences." United Nations arms inspectors were sent back to Iraq. On December 7, 2002, Iran submitted to the United Nations a lengthy declaration stating that it had no weapons that had been banned. In mid-January, United Nations inspectors discovered undeclared empty chemical warheads. This caused doubts to begin to grow, even among those who had supported the Bush drive toward war. During January, President Bush received a letter signed by 130 members of the House of Representatives, urging him to "let the inspectors work." However, by this time, nearly 200,000 United States troops were in the Middle East region, and the dynamic toward conflict was firmly in place. On January 28, 2003, the president delivered his State of the Union address, making the argument that Iraq was attempting to buy uranium from Africa, even though he already had the intelligence that Iraq had not done so (see earlier). By February, United Nations weapons inspector Hans Blix indicated that there was some progress with Iraq's compliance. By March 14, 2003, the Security Council had only four out of the necessary nine votes to support military action.

Demonstrations Against War

On February 15, 2003, "The World Says No to War" protest took place, with massive peace demonstrations around the world. It was the largest coordinated day of protest in world history, with more than 600 cities participating. In Rome alone nearly 3 million people protested, noted in the *Guinness Book of World Records* as the largest antiwar rally in history.

On March 19, 2003, President Bush declared war on Iraq without a United Nations Mandate, as he said he would in his State of the Union address on January 28, and Operation Iraqi Freedom was commenced. Secretary of Defense Donald Rumsfeld addressed concerns about the war, saying, "What will follow will not be a repeat of any other conflict. It will be of a force and a scope and a scale that has been beyond what we have seen before." Officials such as Rumsfeld, Paul Wolfowitz, and Vice President Dick Cheney predicted the conflict would be swift and simple.

OTHER TERRORIST ATTACKS

Although no terrorist outrage on the scale of September 11 has occurred in the United States since that terrible day, there have been several other notable attacks, with varying degrees of success.

- *The shoe bomber.* On December 22, 2001, Richard Reid, a disgruntled supporter of Al-Qaeda, attempted to detonate explosives hidden in his shoe while flying from Paris to Miami. Passengers disabled him, and he was tried, convicted, and sentenced to prison.
- *The underwear bomber.* Umar Farouk Abdulmutallab, a Nigerian/Yemeni man, tried to blow up a Northwest Airlines flight on December 25, 2009, with explosives hidden in his underwear. The bomb did not detonate as planned, and Abdulmutallab was arrested and subsequently convicted and sent to jail.
- *The marathon bombings.* On April 15, 2013, as runners were passing the finish line of the Boston Marathon, two bombs went off nearby, killing 3 people and wounding 264 others. The explosions were the work of two brothers, Dzhokhar and Tamerlan Tsarnaev, from Chechnya in the former Soviet Union. Tamerlan was later killed in a gun battle with police, while Dzhokhar was eventually captured and is awaiting trial.

THE OCCUPATION OF IRAQ

Fiasco and Civil War

The Iraq War in its first phases ended swiftly and as easily as many of its supporters had predicted. Baghdad fell on April 9 to American forces, and Saddam fled into hiding. Almost immediately, though, it became apparent that things were not going as planned.

Despite careful searching, troops and investigators failed to find any of the weapons of mass destruction that had formed the basis for the invasion. The sites mentioned by Colin Powell in his presentation to the UN Security Council turned out to be nonexistent or false information. Embarrassed, the administration tried to change the justification for the invasion, suggesting that even if Saddam didn't actually have weapons of mass destruction, he *wanted* to have them. However, in the end the Iraq invasion proved a major fiasco for the U.S. intelligence community, as well as for the president's advisors who'd planned the war.

In the aftermath of the invasion, an outbreak of looting swept over the city and other cities in Iraq. Priceless antiques were stolen from the National Museum of Iraq. More worrying, enormous quantities of firearms and ammunition were taken.

Words of Wisdom

"Freedom's untidy, and free people are free to make mistakes and commit crimes and do bad things."
—Defense Secretary Donald Rumsfeld, when asked about looting in Baghdad

THE OCCUPATION

Although the U.S. government had hoped that its occupation of Iraq would be short, it soon became obvious this would not be the case. Paul Bremer, who was brought in to oversee the occupation, dissolved the Iraqi army. This left hundreds of thousands of soldiers out of work and angry at the Americans—not to mention having access to a good deal of stolen military equipment. Bremer also barred any former members of Saddam's Ba'athist party from holding office, which excluded many talented administrators from the new government.

An insurgency quickly developed, which began to launch thousands of attacks against the American forces. Bremer's Coalition Provisional Authority closed off a section of Baghdad—the so-called Green Zone—and many of the American civilians stationed in Iraq never dared venture beyond its confines. Private armies of Iraqis quickly formed, and factions multiplied, divided, and reformed.

THE SURGE

By 2007 it was obvious that American military strategy was not working. President Bush authorized a temporary increase in the number of troops, known as "the surge," which he hoped would stabilize the situation. By mid-2008, violence in the country began to subside, although attacks on American troops as well as Iraqi forces loyal to the government continued.

The Bush administration negotiated a Status of Forces Agreement with the Iraqi government that called for all U.S. troops to be out of the country by 2010. This agreement was honored by the administration of Barack Obama, and in August 2010 the last U.S. combat troops left the country. The Iraq War, far from being quick and easy, was one of the longest wars in American history.

Iraqi and American Deaths

A total of about 4,400 U.S. soldiers died during the war; more than 32,000 were injured, many with severe traumatic wounds. Estimates of the number of Iraqis killed vary widely. Some estimate that the number is about 100,000; others suggest the figure could be as high as 600,000.

AFGHAN FIGHTING CONTINUES

Despite the collapse of the Taliban government in Afghanistan, elements of the Taliban continued to battle the forces of the Afghan government as well as the U.S. troops still in the country. By 2014, the Afghan War had become the longest ever fought by American soldiers. Despite continued unrest in the country, President Obama promised to withdraw all but 9,000 American troops by the end of 2014, and remove the rest by the end of 2016.

THE GREAT RECESSION

End of a Bubble

During the closing decade of the twentieth century and the first five or six years of the new millennium, housing prices in the United States continued to rise at a steady clip. As prices soared, homeowners leveraged the value of their property by taking out loans backed by their mortgages.

Others were strongly encouraged by banks and other lending institutions to become homeowners themselves and get in on the rising market. Mortgages were often structured as "adjustable rate mortgages," in which the rate, which remained low at first, would rise sharply at some point. Buyers were often required to make little or no down payments on their homes and were often persuaded to borrow more money than their financial situations warranted.

In short, the United States was in the middle of a housing bubble.

House Flipping

With home prices rising so fast, some homeowners purchased houses for the express purpose of "flipping" them—that is, doing simple, cosmetic upgrades and then reselling the houses at an increased price. So popular was this idea that television shows were built around it.

At the same time, the Fed kept interest rates low while home prices in California, Florida, Arizona, and several other states increased by as much as 10 percent annually. The bubble was dizzying for those involved in it, and as a result many banks engaged in irresponsible—and even borderline illegal—lending practices.

By 2005, the bubble's growth had begun to slow as people's confidence fell. Beginning in February 2007, the slowdown had become a free-range fall. As mortgage rates adjusted higher, families could not keep up their payments and were forced into foreclosure. The number of empty houses on the market rose dramatically, driving down housing prices further.

FINANCIAL MARKETS PLUNGE

For much of the previous decade, regulations on Wall Street firms had been loosened, permitting the evolution of financial "instruments" that no one understood very well. At the heart of this was what were called credit default swaps, essentially a way of spreading the risk of mortgage default among many creditors.

In 2008, the financial system that was filled with these instruments experienced a violent spasm. Major financial institutions suddenly found themselves bankrupt.

Bankruptcies and Crises
- Lehman Brothers (bankrupt)
- Bear Stearns (sold to JPMorgan Chase at a fire-sale price)
- Merrill Lynch (sold to Bank of America at a reduced price)
- American International Group (seized by U.S. government)

As the financial crisis swept through the markets, the New York Stock Exchange plummeted while unemployment rose from 5 percent to 10 percent within a year. Housing prices fell an average of 30 percent, leaving many homeowners owing more on their mortgages than their houses were worth.

THE BAILOUT

The closing months of the Bush administration and the opening of the Obama administration were preoccupied with the Great Recession. Chief among the responses was the Troubled Asset Relief Program (TARP), initiated in October 2008 and designed to fend off bankruptcy from the largest financial institutions.

Too Big?

Among the most important organizations affected by the crisis was the American International Group, a massive insurance company. AIG executives, in making their case to the government, claimed AIG was "too big to fail."

By October 2012, TARP had paid out $432 billion to keep companies afloat and purchase bad assets (mainly mortgages). Although this was less than the program had originally conceived (Treasury Secretary Paulson initially asked for $700 billion), Americans were still angry that this money was spent on companies that had often engaged in unsafe financial maneuvering. Nonetheless, many credit TARP with saving the country from lurching from recession into a full-blown depression.

As a result of various policies designed to encourage employment, over the next six years the country slowly, weakly started to recover from the worst financial crisis since the Great Depression.

BARACK H. OBAMA

Hope and Change

The closing years of George Bush's administration were plagued with problems: the ongoing wars in Iraq and Afghanistan, which dragged on, killing and wounding American soldiers; the growing financial crisis; the government's sluggish response to Hurricane Katrina, which devastated the Gulf Coast in 2005.

Among the Democratic contenders for the presidential nomination, two leaders quickly emerged: Sen. Hillary Clinton of New York and Sen. Barack Obama of Illinois.

A LITTLE-KNOWN CANDIDATE

Thanks to her husband's presidency and her years spent in the limelight, Clinton was well known to voters, and at the outset was favored to win the nomination. Far less was known about Obama, who had been an Illinois state senator before being elected to the U.S. Senate in 2004. That same year he was chosen to deliver the keynote speech at the Democratic National Convention. His power as a speaker made an immediate and powerful impression on the crowd. He appealed to them to hope for a new tomorrow, a theme, he said, that runs through American history.

" . . . It's the hope of slaves sitting around a fire singing freedom songs. The hope of immigrants setting out for distant shores. The hope of a young naval lieutenant bravely patrolling the Mekong

Delta. The hope of a mill worker's son who dares to defy the odds. The hope of a skinny kid with a funny name who believes that America has a place for him, too.

"Hope! Hope in the face of difficulty! Hope in the face of uncertainty! The audacity of hope!..."

The Audacity of Hope

Obama authored two bestselling books before his election as president. One, *Dreams from My Father,* discussed his mixed race heritage and his father, whom he knew only slightly. The other, *The Audacity of Hope*, picked up on the themes from his keynote speech to the Democratic Convention and was a more conventionally political work.

HAWAII, INDONESIA, AND CHICAGO

Obama was born in Honolulu in 1961 to Stanley Ann Dunham of Kansas and Barack Obama Sr. from Kenya. The parents separated about the time of Obama's birth, and he never knew his father. He was raised by his mother and his maternal grandparents; his youth included an extended stay in Indonesia after his mother remarried, this time to an Indonesian graduate student.

Obama returned to Honolulu in 1971 and grew up in Hawaii. He attended college in Los Angeles and then transferred to Columbia in New York City. After graduating, he moved to Chicago to become a community organizer.

After several years of working in Chicago's south side, Obama entered Harvard Law School and became the editor of the *Harvard Law Review*. He maintained his ties to Chicago, and after graduating Harvard, he moved there with his wife, Michelle.

SENATOR OBAMA

Obama's political ambitions were never concealed; they were fueled by his work with community organizations. In 1997 he ran for state senator and won; in Springfield he began learning the art of writing and passing legislation. In 2002 he announced his candidacy for U.S. senator from Illinois. His victory catapulted him to national prominence as one of the few African-American senators. This status was confirmed by the success of his speech to the Democratic National Convention in 2004.

Community Organizing

During the 1960s and 1970s, many local neighborhood organizations sprang up, aiming at improving living conditions. The groups dealt with such problems as sanitation, safety, tenants' rights, and other practical issues of day-to-day life. The dean of this kind of organizing was the Chicagoan Saul Alinsky, who laid out his methods in his book *Rules for Radicals*.

THE PRESIDENTIAL CAMPAIGN

Obama's decision to run for president in 2008 caught many by surprise, since it had been assumed he would remain in the Senate for some time before trying for higher office. His campaign was greatly aided by media-savvy organizers who took advantage of the new phenomenon of social media to spread news of his campaign activities. In November 2008 he defeated the Republican candidate, Sen. John McCain, becoming the first African-American president in U.S. history.

INDEX